Vegetarian Everyday

Vegetarian Everyday

Healthy Recipes from Our Green Kitchen

David Frenkiel & Luise Vindahl

RIZZOLI
NEW YORK

New York Paris London Milan

Contents

Introduction

The moment we met, our two food worlds collided.
I was the unhealthy vegetarian (yes, they do exist) who
basically lived on pasta, pizza, sweets and ice cream.
And Luise was a very health-conscious meat eater,
who had practically scratched those foods from her
repertoire. After a couple of awkward months (huge
understatement), we made a decision. We realized that
if we were to be able to live together, I had to learn
about whole grains, quinoa and natural sweeteners,
while Luise decided to start cutting down on meat and
experimenting with vegetable-based meals. And instead
of focusing on all the things we didn't eat, we
did the opposite.

All of a sudden we found ourselves discussing how
to cook a dinner that put the vegetables in focus, and
was still nourishing enough to eat after a long day or a
workout. We filled our home with fruit, vegetables, nuts,
seeds, whole grains and good fats and decided to start
cooking food and baking cakes that were healthy and
green, without being boring.

One of the first things we made was a carrot cake,
where you could actually feel the texture and taste of
the carrots, not just the sugar in it. And we made baked
herb falafel that we wrapped in thin, crunchy cabbage
leaves instead of plain, dry pita bread. We also learned to
appreciate simple things like a freshly squeezed vegetable
juice, which tastes sweeter than anything you can buy
in the supermarket, yet contains no sugar at all. The
possibilities seemed endless and everything we made
tasted so much better than it had ever done before.
As a way of documenting our food endeavors (and
failures) we bought a camera, registered the blog

Green Kitchen Stories, and started writing. And that is what we have been doing for more than three years now. This book is a resume of what we have learned and perhaps a guide, of sorts, to our way of eating.

To help you get the full picture, we will rewind the tape a couple of years. Our story started late at night on a small dance floor not more than 10 meters from the river Tiber and 20 meters from Castel Sant'Angelo, in central Rome. That is where we met and fell in love six years ago. I don't think the subject of food came up once during our first conversation (strange considering that we were in Italy and everybody ALWAYS talks about food there). But I know for a fact that we talked about it on our first date one week later. I was so nervous that I memorized 20 questions, to avoid having nothing to say. And after having lived in Rome for six months, 15 of those questions were food-related. It didn't take us long to realize that we had two vastly different approaches to food.

I have been a vegetarian since I was 15-years-old. It has never been a radical choice for me. I am not a meat-hater. I have just chosen to eat vegetables instead. It makes me feel better in every way possible. I can sit around a table with people eating steaks, without commenting or even thinking about it. But I do expect the same treatment back. What I eat is my choice; please spare me any ironic comments. Although I enjoyed spending time in the kitchen before I met Luise, the largest part of my plate was always filled with pasta, potatoes, bread and white rice.

Luise has always been a cautious eater. She makes lots of deliberately healthy choices that for some might seem complicated, but for her makes perfect sense. She has always had an active lifestyle, and eating well is an essential part of that. She eats some fish and organic poultry occasionally, but has become amazingly creative in turning a few vegetables into a feast. For her, health is not only about eating green, she is also very interested in herbal medicine and natural remedies. And she obviously must be doing something right, because I have never met a person who looks so healthy and recovers so quickly from a virus.

Today we live in a crammed but charming apartment in Stockholm, Sweden, with our daughter, Elsa. Although we both have careers of our own, and none of us have any professional background in cooking, food has become something we talk about from early morning to late evening.

We try to eat as varied a diet as possible at home. That is why our recipes are sometimes raw and other times cooked. Sometimes they call for buckwheat, which is gluten-free, and other times for spelt, which is not. Many of our recipes are vegan, but we love to eat eggs and cheese every now and then. Look into our kitchen and you will not only notice all the nuts that Elsa has spread over the floor, but also the wide array of whole flours, dried fruit, seeds, superfoods and multi-colored quinoa that we keep in our cupboard. Open our fridge and you will probably be attacked by an organic and locally harvested cabbage. It's usually so big that we throw it in just before closing the door, thus it is also the first thing that jumps out when you open it. Behind it you might find some more seasonal vegetables (organic, when not too expensive), seven million jars of nut butters and spreads, a goat's yogurt and three different versions of plant milk, usually oat, almond and rice. Even though it might sound like a parody, this is an exact description of how our kitchen looks right now. We don't have a perfect and clean home, but we do love whole foods.

This book is filled with recipes from our everyday life, along with some simple tips on how to get a more varied and greener pantry. We want to keep it simple, basic and very useful. Here we have shared the kind of food that we often eat at home. Not all our recipes can be whipped together in 20 minutes, but many of them can (a few in even less time). Some of them will take hours, but they are worth it. We have tried to make sure that there will be lots of recipes to choose from (or adapt) if you are vegan or have any allergies. More than 90% of the recipes in this book are, by the way, gluten-free.

We have divided the book into Mornings (where you will find breakfasts both for a stressful Tuesday and a weekend brunch); Lighter Meals (suitable for lunches and effortless dinners throughout the week); Family Dinners (perfect for a larger weekend gatherings); Good to Go (dishes that will survive a few hours in a picnic basket); Small Bites (for a buffet table or as a side dish); Drinks (from fresh juices to Indian chai tea); and Sweets & Treats (to trigger your sweet tooth, even though naturally sweetened with fruit and full of whole grains).

We find food inspiration from all over the world. Of course we read a lot of blogs, but our little family has also travelled around the world together. You can probably trace which countries we have visited, just by looking at the recipe index. One country that we always return to is Italy, and you will definitely notice the influence in how we use oil, lemon and fresh herbs. Apart from that, we have also thrown a little bit of our Scandinavian heritage into this book. A classic dark Danish rye bread, a Swedish hash pan, a cold Danish berry soup, a curried egg salad, a mouth-watering pancake cake and delicious thin crisp bread. We have included recipes that most Scandinavian families have their own versions of, but with our own twist. Most of the recipes are written solely for this book, but we have also included our favorites from the blog. They have new photos and many of them have also been altered in different ways – new flavors have been added, the methods have been perfected or there are new suggestions of what to serve them with. So even though you might recognize a recipe, it might be worth trying it again.

Luise and I have written this book and developed all the recipes together. Both our voices will guide you through it (and sometimes also the voice of our daughter). We hope that you will find many new favorite recipes, but also that we can inspire you to pursue your own way into the world of whole foods.

INTRODUCTION

Inside Our Pantry

Although the ingredients we have in our kitchen are constantly shifting, there are a large number of items that we make sure to keep on hand. Here we have organized them in lists, with short explanations of each product – use this as our guide for stocking your own Green Kitchen. With these ingredients at home, you will not only be ready to try most of the recipes in this book, but also ready to start doing some improvising yourself. Creating a greener, healthier and more versatile pantry really makes a difference in helping to improve your eating habits: You're more likely to bake with natural sweeteners or whole grains if you already have them on hand. It can be more expensive to buy organic products, whole grains, nuts and seeds, so don't feel obliged to get all of them at once; just make sure you have a few ingredients in each category.

BUTTER, VINEGAR AND OIL

Being on the healthy track doesn't mean avoiding fat, quite the opposite. It is highly important. But of course it matters what kind of oils and fats you choose, which you heat and which you use raw. Here are our favorites.

Butter

Adds great taste to cookies and sweets. We sometimes replace it with the more neutral coconut oil. Choose organic butter from grass-fed cows if you can.

Ghee (clarified butter)

Very delicious raw, but also perfect for frying because of its high smoke point. Use for both sweet and savory food. To make ghee see the recipe on page 25.

Apple cider vinegar

Our favorite vinegar, it has a fruity and sour taste and is cheaper than many other vinegars. Great in salad dressings.

Balsamic vinegar

A dark vinegar with a rich smooth, sweet and sour taste.

Red and white wine vinegar

Perfect in salads and marinades.

Rice vinegar

Good in Asian food and, of course, rice. We use it in our Sushi Explosion on page 132.

Cold-pressed flax oil

High in omega-3 and -6, which are important for vegans. We mainly use it in smoothies.

Extra virgin coconut oil/butter

Sold with or without coconut flavor. It has a high smoke point, so is ideal for frying. Liquid or "creamy" at room temperature and solid when kept in the fridge. We often use it in raw desserts.

Extra virgin olive oil

Best used raw or heated at low temperatures. We use stronger flavored olive oils in salads or drizzled over our pizza, and milder ones for frying and baking.

Extra virgin rapeseed (canola) oil

Very common in Scandinavia. Has a nice nutty taste and is perfect in baked goods.

Unrefined sesame oil

A very flavorful oil, you often need only a few drops. Good in Asian food. We use it for marinating tofu, in salads and noodle dishes.

NUTS AND SEEDS

Look inside our pantry and you will find an almost frightening amount of nuts and seeds. We are true addicts and use them in everything from breakfasts, salads, dinners and desserts. They are rich in proteins, good fats and minerals, and therefore very important in a vegetarian diet.

Almonds

Contain a high amount of good fat. Can be turned into nut butter easily. We use them toasted in salads, granola and desserts.

Amaranth

An even smaller gluten-free seed than quinoa, but slightly higher in protein. We have stuffed tomatoes with cooked amaranth on page 152.

Brazil nuts

We love them soaked as a snack or in our Breakfast Blend on page 46.

Cashew nuts

A sweet and rich nut. Good for soaking and making raw cream or raw cheese.

Dried and shredded or flaked coconut

Good in breakfasts, baking, smoothies and soups.

Flax seeds (Linseeds)

Brown or golden, rich in omega-3 fatty acid. We add to desserts, bread and smoothies to make them more nutritious.

Hazelnuts

Great with both sweet and savory food. Try the Hazelnut, Eggplant & Mushroom parcels on page 126.

Hemp seeds

Although this seed is a relative of Marijuana, it doesn't get you high. It has a nutty, almost sweet taste and is packed with protein and a wide variety of minerals and vitamins. Makes good plant milk, but even better as a raw topping on muesli.

Hulled buckwheat

A gluten-free, 3-d triangular seed. We use it in our Buckwheat & Ginger Porridge on page 57.

Macadamia nuts

Crispy white nuts. Delicious on their own and in chocolate desserts.

Nut and seed butters

Perfect as a bread spread, on porridge, in smoothies and in raw chocolate mousse. We usually keep several different varieties at home. Our favorites are peanut, tahini (sesame), almond, sunflower and apricot kernel.

Pine nuts

Expensive little nuts and pesto's best friend.

Pistachio nuts

Not only our favorite ice cream flavor, also wonderful in muffins and in savory food together with goat cheese.

Psyllium seeds

Good in gluten-free baking. They bind moisture and help make bread less crumbly.

Pumpkin seeds

This seed adds an extra dimension to everything from granola to soups and salads. They have a slight grainy texture when raw, crunchy when roasted.

Quinoa (red, white and black)

A gluten-free super-seed, packed with protein and fiber. Different colors have slightly different tastes. Beautiful in salads.

Sunflower seeds

Contain less fat than nuts and are less allergenic. David's favorite seed – he uses it a lot in baking and desserts. We often give them a quick roast to enhance the flavor. Check out the crust on our Frozen Strawberry Cheesecake on page 218.

Walnuts

Same shape as a brain and that is exactly what they are good for. Good in baking.

DRIED BEANS, LENTILS AND PEAS

Pulses are the vegetarian's number one source of protein. They are rich in fiber and high in minerals, vitamins and complex carbohydrates, and are a really cheap source of protein. Buy large bags of dried beans, peas and lentils, soak, cook and freeze in portions and you'll always have an easy meal at hand. Cooking instructions on page 28.

Adzuki beans

These flavorful small beans are also known as the "weight loss bean." They are good in "chili sin carne" or other bean stews.

Beluga and Puy lentils

Beautiful looking and wonderful flavors. Hold together better than red and yellow lentils. We serve them as an alternative to rice and pasta.

Black beans

Most common bean in Latin American cooking. Try our Savoy Tacos with Corn and Mango on page 82.

Black-yellow-eyed beans

Cream-colored beans with a characteristic black or yellow spot or "eye." Dressed lightly in olive oil, lemon and herbs, they make a delicious salad.

Borlotti beans

If you have the opportunity to get these beans fresh, they are incredibly beautiful. Great in soups.

Butter (Lima) beans

Large white bean, perfect in a mixed bean salad, and they add a silky creaminess to soups.

Cannellini beans

Small white bean. Good as a spread on bread or in our bean version of a risotto on page 146.

Chickpeas (Garbanzo beans)

Elsa's favorite. Leave a bowl of boiled chickpeas in front of her, and they will be gone within minutes. We use them in salads, soups (page 81) and hummus.

Navy beans

This small white bean has a sweet flavor and can be used as an alternative to cannellini beans.

Kidney beans

Kidney-shaped, of course, and sweet in taste. Great in spicy stews.

Mung beans

Beautiful color and Luise's favorite sprouting bean. Try the sprouted mung bean Sprout Ceviche on page 167.

Pinto beans

Pinto means "painted" in Spanish which is what they look like. We use them as a bruschetta topping.

Red, yellow and green lentils

Great in soups and in Indian food. Try our Sweet Apricot & Cauliflower Dal on page 115.

Tofu

Made from soy beans. Nice warm or cold and perfect for making a dish more filling. Choose organic non-GMO if possible.

Yellow and green split peas

Sweeter and creamier than lentils. Try our Rhubarb, Apple & Yellow Split Pea Stew on page 116.

PLANT-BASED MILK AND CREAM

The milk debate has heated up in the last couple of years and a lot has been said for and against, so let's not bore you with more of that. Instead we have listed our favorite milks and creams. Most can be used as a straight substitute for dairy milk but use soy or coconut milk if you need to heat it. There are many good kinds to try so start tasting.

Coconut milk

A natural-fat plant milk. Used commonly in Indian stews, but we also use it in desserts, ice creams and shakes.

Goat's milk

Thick and creamy and usually available from small farms, although some supermarkets and health food stores do stock it.

Hemp milk

Homemade sweetened hemp milk is much better than store-bought, which can be a little bitter.

Nut milk

Make your own by following our recipe on page 27.

Oat cream, soy cream and nut cream

Great nondairy alternatives to regular cream. Buy in-store or see our recipe on page 27.

Oat milk

The one we most often keep at home, because it's easy to get in Sweden and less expensive than, for example, almond milk. If you can't find any, make your own by following our recipe on page 27.

Rice milk

We use it in smoothies; it is a bit sweeter than oat milk.

Soy milk

Great for heating and making foam.

NATURAL SWEETENERS

Although we have recipes for indulgent desserts, decadent cakes and sweet drinks you won't find sugar anywhere in this book (apart from in the recipe to make your own Bubbling Kombucha Cocktail on page 184). A few years ago we started moving to more natural alternatives to sweeten our recipes. Today we don't even keep regular sugar at home. It was a challenge for us in the beginning but now we really appreciate the natural flavors of these sweeteners.

Apple syrup, juice and unsweetened sauce
Pure apples that are pressed into a juice and boiled down to a syrup are great in fruit juices, granolas and baking, but also in marinades. Apple sauce can be used as a sweetener or to replace eggs in cakes. Both are easy to make at home. See page 30.

Bananas
Use to sweeten shakes and smoothies, but also fruitier cakes. Can be substituted with very ripe pears.

Birch sugar (natural xylitol)
Dissolves quickly and looks and tastes similar to sugar. Only use small amounts. We mix it with cinnamon and drizzle over rice porridge.

Coconut palm sugar
Looks very similar to granulated sugar; it has a caramel-like taste and is great in cookies.

Dried unsulphured apricots and prunes
Truly good sweeteners in stews, compotes, porridge and jam.

Fresh and dried dates, and date syrup
Very sweet. Good to mix with nuts into delicious vegan cakes, crusts and truffles. Raw Date Syrup (see page 30) is a great substitute for agave, honey, maple syrup and yacon syrup.

Pure maple syrup
When Elsa was born, a blog reader sent us a bottle of pure maple syrup from Canada and we have been in love with it ever since. We use it in baking, on pancakes, waffles, porridge or oatmeal.

Raw honey and clear honey
We are so lucky to have friends who provide us with delicious raw honey. Honey contains antioxidants, minerals and vitamins and is therefore a great natural sweetener. Try a morning shot – add it to hot water, ginger, lemon and ghee.

Vanilla extract, vanilla beans or ground vanilla
We love vanilla. It gives desserts a sweet and distinctive touch.

PASTA AND NOODLES

There are many more nutritious and flavorful varieties than the traditional wheat noodle. They come in many colors, tastes and shapes.

Kelp noodles
A sea vegetable made into raw noodles. Neutral in flavor. Easy to toss in a tasty dressing.

Udon rice, and soba buckwheat noodles
Good gluten-free varieties. Great in Asian salads or spicy coconut soups.

Whole-grain and gluten-free pasta
Available in many varieties like corn, spelt, buckwheat and rice.

Whole-grain lasagna
We often use zucchini, sweet potato or eggplant slices instead, but when we don't, we use whole-grain lasagna noodles.

FLOURS AND GRAINS

When we started using wholewheat flour instead of white (all-purpose) flour, it was because it produced more healthful bread and desserts. But after learning more about the different qualities, textures and flavors of each flour we realized that we now bake more flavorful and interesting cakes, bread and pancakes than we ever did before. Many of our flours are gluten-free, but not all of them.

Almond flour

Gluten-free and wonderful to use in pie and tart shells. Adds a sweet nuttiness to everything. Make it yourself by simply grinding raw almonds into a fine powdered flour, or buy ready-made.

Baking powder and baking soda

Essential in muffins, scones and all baked goods that don't call for leavening.

Brown rice flour

A gluten-free flour with a nutty flavor. Good in baking. We often use it combined with other flours.

Buckwheat flour

Gluten-free with an earthy flavor. We use to make pancakes and crepes, but it is also good in muffins.

Chestnut flour

Gluten-free. Available from most healthfood stores. It has an incredibly nutty flavor and is good in crepes, breads and cakes.

Chickpea (Garbanzo) flour

One of our favorite gluten-free flours. Good mixed with almond flour in pie and tart cases, and also for making pancakes.

Cornflour (Cornstarch)

Fine-ground, white powdered maize used for thickening and baking.

Cornmeal

Gluten-free with a distinct corn taste. Great for making tortillas, cornbread or our savory muffins on page 95.

Kamut flour

Kamut is a nutritious whole grain in the wheat family. It is a better alternative than regular wheat flour.

Quinoa flour

Gluten-free and rich in protein. Makes moist baked goods.

Rye flour

Dark grain that we use in rye bread, pancake batters, cookies and crispbread. Not very elastic and difficult to knead, therefore more suited to looser batters and doughs.

Spelt flour

Ancient cousin to wheat. Less refined, with more fibers and less gluten (although not gluten-free). Mild and sweet flavor, it is our favorite flour to bake with. Good elasticity and leavening. Don't knead it too long, or it can become crumbly.

Wheatgerm

A powerhouse of nutrition. You can use it to replace one half to one cup of the flour in baking. Use it in pancakes, waffles, bread and cookies.

Fresh and active dry yeast

Most of our bread and pizza recipes use dry yeast because we always have it at home. But you can use fresh yeast instead. Follow instructions on the packet for use.

Arrowroot

A natural starch. Use in baking, and to thicken stews, desserts and soups. Don't continue to cook after it thickens or it goes runny again. We use it in our Beet Bourguignon recipe on page 121.

Millet

Gluten-free and rich in fiber and protein. We use it as a gluten-free couscous replacer or mash it together with cauliflower for a side dish.

Polenta

Gluten-free coarse-ground cornmeal. Use to accompany a dinner instead of mashed potatoes.

Can also be cooked with cinnamon and nut milk for a sweet version.

Rice – red, black, brown, wild

Gluten-free. The varieties of colors, flavors and textures are amazing and so much healthier than refined white rice. Wild rice is actually a grass.

Rolled oats

Use in baked oatmeal and crunchy cookies. Can be used as an egg-free binder in veggie burgers and polpette. Many oats have traces of gluten, but you can buy gluten-free rolled oats.

Rye berry, wheat berry, spelt berry and barley

Come as entire kernels (without the husk). Soak and cook with herbs or spices and they'll make your salad into a feast. Good in stews and in bread, too. Try the Dark Danish Rye Bread on page 58.

Whole-grain couscous

Wheat grain, often served with North African dishes and good in salads. Try with our Moroccan Vegetable Tagine on page 125.

SUPERFOODS

We use these products to add nutrition to smoothies, desserts or baked goods. They'll give your body a concentrated amount of high nutrients. Some of these might be very expensive and others quite cheap, depending on where in the world you live, so go and have a look in your local healthfood store.

Açai powder

Beautiful purple berry from South America. Contains more antioxidants than blueberries. Only sold frozen or dried and can be difficult to find. We mostly use it in smoothies or blends.

Bee pollen

Small yellow/orange granules. Naturally good together with honey. Sweet tasting and perfect in smoothies. Looks pretty when sprinkled over porridge and desserts.

Carob powder

Looks similar to cacao and is good combined with it. The taste is slightly different, but still sweet. Rich in calcium. We add it to chocolate mousse or use in baking.

Chia seeds

A power seed even more nutritious than flax seed, but also more expensive. We often use these as an egg substitute in baking, or in our smoothies.

Dried goji, inca, mulberries, cranberries

Antioxidant-rich superberries; choose organic if possible.

Dried nettles

Packed with iron. Buy in healthfood stores or hang fresh nettles up until dry and then crush them by hand. We use in smoothies, porridge, pancakes, bread and tea.

Hemp, pea or brown rice protein powder

Nutritious natural protein powders, great in your morning smoothie or post-workout drink. Also great for children's "I-refuse-to-eat" phases.

Nori sheets

Seaweed made from the red algae. We use when making sushi, nori rolls and sushi salad. To be honest, this is the only algae we are crazy about.

Raw cacao powder and nibs

High-quality superfood. High in magnesium and very rich in antioxidants. Great in raw desserts.

Rosehip powder

Made from dried rosehip. Very high in vitamin C. Tastes like fruit and flowers. We love it in baked cakes and breads and on our morning yogurt.

Spirulina powder

A blue-green micro algae. Add a spoonful to drinks or make the Spirulina Chocolate Truffles on page 232.

Wheatgrass powder

Very healthful. Often used in holistic medicine for regenerating cells. We often mix it with lemon to neutralize the flavor. Try our Green Cleanse Power Shot on page 193.

FERMENTED ESSENTIALS

Fermented food contains natural probiotics (a type of living bacteria), which are essential to our overall health and wellbeing. It is the best medicine for the digestive system.

Kimchi

Fermented Chinese cabbage with lots of hot chili. We use it in stews to add an Asian twist. David makes his own, but you can buy it in Asian stores.

Kombucha

Fermented bubbling tea. We always keep a kombucha "mushroom" ready in a jar. See page 184.

Miso

Asian paste made from fermented beans or grains. Use it in soups, spreads or sauces. Not all miso pastes are vegetarian. Choose organic and non-GMO if you can get it.

Sauerkraut

Lacto-fermented white cabbage. Super-healthy and perfect for a topping on stews or as a sandwich filling.

Sourdough

Natural leavening and lactic acid fermentation is why sourdough makes the most healthful bread you can find. Good with rye flour.

Soy sauce and tamari

Asian sauce made from fermented bean or grain paste; choose organic and non-GMO if possible.

KITCHEN APPLIANCES

Our kitchen has limited space, so we have only invested in a few appliances that we can use for almost everything. For example, we don't have an electric bread machine which is why the instructions in all our bread recipes are by hand. If using a machine you can of course skip the kneading step.

Blender

After working our way through a couple of cheaper brands we finally bought a Vitamix. It is one of the most powerful blenders on the market and can easily purée nuts into perfectly smooth nut butter or nut milk, and make all smoothies thick and creamy.

Hand (immersion) blender and food processor

Our most-used kitchen machine. Although I had a pretty nasty accident with this, we still use it almost every day. We use the hand blender for soups and smoothies and then connect it to a food processor that we use to make pesto and grind nuts.

Electric juicer

Although a hassle to clean, we use our juicer surprisingly often to turn week-old vegetables and fruit into sweet juice, instead of throwing them away. Turn to page 188 for juicing tips.

Kitchen scales

Scales are the only way to make sure that the measurements are correct when baking. Digital works best, since you can reset it to use with different containers.

Mortar and pestle

Great for grinding spices and making pestos. Freshly ground spices taste more intense flavor than store-bought.

Healthy Start

When Elsa was born, food became even more important to us. We knew from the start that we wanted her to eat the same things we did. When starting to plan this book, we discussed including a chapter with children's food, but the more we thought about it, we realized that from the moment we started Elsa on solid foods, she has actually been eating the same things that we eat. And it has worked so well, that instead of sharing special children's recipes, we'll just give you our best tips on how to give your kids a good and healthy start to eating well. These things have worked for us and for Elsa, so hopefully they will be helpful for you, too.

Start as you mean to go on . . .

Try to reduce or eliminate gluten and dairy products during your baby's first year or two. They can be hard to digest for anyone, but especially for young children. Even if they have no allergies or food intolerances, many people react to these food irritants. No sugar during your baby's first years. Sugar tastes good but has lots of downsides – it causes hyper-activity, weakens the immune system and can lead to cavities, just to mention a few. We also have our own personal theory about sugar: Once you start offering sweets, it will be harder to get children to try things that are not sweet. The longer you prolong the introduction of sugar, the more your children will be open to trying new foods and eating their greens, which makes life a whole lot easier for you.

"One ice cream every now and then won't hurt her." You wouldn't believe how many times we heard that sentence. And sure, they are right, she eats an ice cream and life goes on. But why? Until she was two years old, Elsa never asked for ice cream herself, she didn't even know what it was. During a child's first two years we as adults choose what food our children should eat and they learn from this – it's our responsibility. If someone wants to give your baby an ice cream, it's probably not because your baby asks for it, it's because they want to give it to her. It's worth thinking about.

If you are vegetarian, we recommend that you raise your children to be the same until they are old enough to express their own opinion. Why give your child something that you wouldn't eat yourself? They will get plenty of proteins, fats, vitamins and minerals from vegetables, eggs, cheese, oils, fruit, beans, lentils, seeds and nuts. You can also add a vitamin and mineral supplement for small children.

8 tips on how to give your children a healthy start in life:

AGREE
Talk everything through with your partner so you both agree on why you are doing this. If you don't agree, every dinner will be an issue. Also discuss with your families and close friends to help them out with food suggestions. Otherwise, they might not dare invite you or your child for dinner any more . . .

KEEP IT SIMPLE
Don't make your and your child's eating habits too difficult to maintain. Figure out what you and your family can live with. We decided that Elsa could eat fish when she stays with other families or in day care, even though we don't eat it at home. It makes life easier for everyone, plus she get lots of good fats and proteins from it.

BE A GOOD ROLE MODEL
The most important thing is not what food you put in front of your children, but what you eat yourself. That is what your children will want to eat as well. We rarely make special food for Elsa and we would never eat an ice cream in front of her if we weren't prepared to give her one, too.

EXPERIMENT WITH SHAPE & TEXTURE
If a child does not like a certain food, try to cook it in different ways. It is not always the taste that children don't like, but sometimes the shape or texture.

BOOST THEIR FAVORITE FOOD
A simple trick to get extra minerals and vitamins in your children's diet is to add superfood ingredients to their favorite foods. Add vegetable juice, for example, when making bread or muffins. Blend spinach in pancake batter or broccoli, nettle powder or linseeds in berry smoothies and porridge (they won't taste it).

ALWAYS HAVE A SNACK AT HAND
A difficulty with healthy eating habits is when your children see other children eating something and they want the same. It can be anything from a hot dog to sweets. We learned early on to always carry a snack or fruit with us, so we can offer her that instead. If you look into Elsa's backpack you will probably always find a hard boiled egg, a carrot, a piece of fruit or some Quinoa & Cauliflower Cakes (page 71).

KEEP CALM
If you see your child with a cookie, don't get hysterical and take it away. It will only make your child want it more. It's only food and it is important to develop a natural relationship with unhealthy food, too.

ENCOURAGE EATING
We have been very laid-back about table manners. As long as she eats, we don't mind if it's with a fork, a spoon, a chopstick, a straw or her hands (soup can get pretty messy). The good part is that she eats (almost) anything that we put in front of her. If you set up too many rules around eating you will probably end up with a food strike.

HEALTHY START

Basic Methods

We have listed a few basic recipes and methods here for things that we often make ourselves. Everything from a simple tomato sauce, which you will have use for in many of the savory recipes in this book, to how to make a simple date syrup that can be used to replace other syrups, honey and molasses in most recipes. You can buy most of these foods at supermarkets or healthfood stores, and we do that ourselves from time to time, but by making them yourself, you get to decide what to put in them.

VEGETABLE STOCK
Makes about 6 pints/15 cups

2 tbsp extra virgin olive oil
2 onions, quartered, unpeeled
3 garlic cloves, unpeeled
2 carrots, chopped
2 leeks, chopped
1 fennel bulb, chopped
1 celery rib, chopped
10–20 flat-leaf parsley stems
4 bay leaves
5 black or white peppercorns
2 tsp sea salt

Heat the oil in a stockpot on medium heat. Add the onions, garlic, carrots, leeks, fennel and celery. Sauté for 3–5 minutes until lightly browned and soft. Add the parsley, bay leaves, pepper, salt and 7 pints/ 16 cups water. Bring to a boil, then lower the heat to very low, cover and gently simmer for about 1 hour or longer if you have time. Taste and adjust seasoning if necessary. Strain the stock and leave to cool, stirring occasionally. Measure out 1 or 2 cup portions and keep in containers in the freezer for up to 6 months. Keeps in the fridge for 1 week.

BASIC TOMATO SAUCE
Makes about 1 quart (4 cups)

2 tbsp extra virgin olive oil
1 yellow onion, finely chopped
2 garlic cloves, finely chopped
½ tsp dried red pepper flakes
3 x 14 oz cans whole plum tomatoes
5 sprigs of basil, leaves picked
sea salt
freshly ground black pepper

Heat the olive oil in a saucepan on medium heat. Add the onion, garlic and red pepper flakes and sauté for a couple of minutes until golden. Stir in the tomatoes, basil, salt and pepper. Use a wooden spoon to crush the tomatoes. Lower the heat, cover and gently simmer for about 20 minutes. Use immediately or cool and store in an airtight glass jar in the fridge (keeps for about 1 week).

BASIC METHODS

GHEE (CLARIFIED BUTTER)
Makes about 1½ cups

1 lb unsalted butter

You will also need:
1 piece of cheesecloth/muslin or a sieve
1 airtight, heatproof glass jar

Heat the butter in a heavy saucepan over medium heat until it has melted. Do not cover the pan. Lower the heat as much as possible and let gently simmer until foam rises to the top of the melted butter. The butter will make lots of sputtering, which means that the butter is boiling, and 3 layers will develop: a white top layer, a liquid yellow layer, and a milk solids bottom layer. This takes about 15–20 minutes. Stir every now and then with a wooden spoon to keep the solids from sticking to the bottom. When the butter is done it will smell like freshly baked croissants and turn to a clear golden yellow color with a little white foam floating on top. Remove from the heat immediately or it will burn.

Place a few layers of cloth or a sieve over the glass jar and carefully pour the hot liquid butter through into the glass. Leave to cool and solidify before closing the airtight lid. Store in the fridge for up to one year, or at room temperature for 3 months.

Tip: You can use all kind of herbs and spices to flavor or color your ghee. Add when the butter is melted and leave it until the end of the process. Try garlic, ginger, cardamom or cumin.

SUPER SIMPLE YOGURT
Serves 2

½ cup plain yogurt with active cultures
   (or from a previous batch of homemade yogurt)
4¼ cups non-homogenized whole milk

You will also need:
1 thermometer for liquids (such as a candy thermometer)

Gently heat the milk to 180°F then allow it to cool to 110°F. Stir in the yogurt and transfer the mixture into a large glass container. Cover the container with a kitchen towel or plate and put in a warm place 150°F, such as a heated (but turned-off) oven or the airing cupboard, and let it sit overnight, or wrap the container with towels. In the morning the yogurt will have grown and thickened. Transfer to glass jars and refrigerate. When the yogurt is cold, serve it. Keeps for 3–5 days in the fridge.

Tip: Use the kind of yogurt and milk you prefer; sheep, cow, goat, soy, almond milk, etc.

Tip: If you prefer a thicker yogurt, you can strain it.

Tip: You can add any flavor you like – spices, herbs or fruits – when the yogurt has grown and thickened.

HOMEMADE NUT OR OAT MILK
Makes 3 cups

1 cup raw nuts (almonds, hazelnuts or
   cashew nuts, etc.) or 1 cup whole oat groats
a pinch of sea salt
1 tsp spices of your choice (cardamom
   seeds, vanilla bean, cinnamon sticks,
   cloves, etc.)

You will also need:
1 piece of cheesecloth/muslin or a fine sieve
1 large glass container

Start by soaking the nuts or oat grouts: place them in a bowl or jar, cover with twice as much water and leave to soak for 6–8 hours or overnight.
Rinse well and place in a blender with 3 cups water and a pinch of salt. Blend on high speed for about a minute. Place the cloth or sieve over the glass container and pour the blended mixture into it. Strain the milk until only the pulp is left. Use your hands to squeeze out the last drops of milk.
Add spices, if you wish, and place in the fridge for about an hour. Drink it, use it in smoothies or pour it over your porridge. The milk keeps for about three days in an airtight container in the fridge.

Tip: To make your own nut cream, follow the instructions for milk, but halve the amount of water.

HOMEMADE NUT & SEED BUTTER
Makes about 2 cups

10½ oz/2 cups raw nuts or seeds
   of choice
1 tsp sea salt
1 tsp ground spice of choice (optional)

Preheat the oven to 275°F. Spread the nuts on a baking sheet and roast in the oven for 20 minutes, or until golden. Remove from oven and cool slightly. If the nuts have skins, tip them off the tray onto a clean tea towel and rub gently to remove the skins.
Add the nuts, salt and spices (if using) to a high-speed blender or food processor and purée for about 3–5 minutes. Depending on how powerful your machine is, this could take even longer. Stop regularly to scrape down the sides. Keep puréeing until the nuts turn into a smooth and creamy paste. Scrape into an airtight container and refrigerate. Keeps for about a month.

Tip: You can make raw nut butter by skipping the roasting step, but it requires a high-speed blender. It will take a little longer for the nuts to release their oils and become a smooth butter. Add sweetener, spices, herbs or superfood of any kind to this recipe. Add towards the end of processing the nuts.

Tip: If you would like the butter to be creamier, add 1–2 tablespoons of a neutral oil, such as cold-pressed safflower, sunflower or grapeseed, while blending.

HOW TO MAKE FRESH SPROUTS

You can either use store-bought sprouting jars
or to make your own you will need:
1 glass jar
1 piece of cheesecloth/muslin or clean nylon stocking
1 rubber band

Ingredients:
1 part dried beans, lentils or seeds
2–3 parts water

Soaking times:

Green lentils, red lentils, black lentils: 8 hrs

Mung beans, adzuki, chickpeas, corn: 8–12 hrs

Buckwheat, amaranth: 30 minutes

Sesame, fenugreek, broccoli, alfalfa, pumpkin
  (pepita) seeds: 8 hrs

Wheat, spelt, rye, oat, barley, kamut, millet, rice: 7–12 hrs

Yellow peas, green peas: 8–12 hrs

Sunflower seeds, quinoa: 2 hrs

Almond, hazelnut, walnut, pecan, cashew nut
  (these nuts do not show a sprouting tail and are
  therefore called "soaks" instead of "sprouts"): 4–8 hrs

Brazil, macadamia, pistachio, pine nut, hemp seeds:
  do not need to soak unless your recipe requires it.

Rinse your seeds in a sieve under cold running water,
then pick out any imperfect seeds.

Transfer your seeds into the sprouting jar/s.

Add 2–3 times as much fresh water and cover with the
screen lid or cheesecloth and rubber band. Leave to
soak (see soaking times).

Drain off the liquid. Rinse the seeds until the water
runs clear and drain very thoroughly. Set your
sprouting jars in a bright place (out of direct sunlight)
at room temperature. Rinse and drain the contents a
couple of times a day. They are ready in 1–3 days or
when the sprouting tail is as long as the seed.

Store in sealed containers in the fridge and use within
1–2 weeks.

HOW TO COOK BEANS

1 cup dried beans
3 cups water for soaking, plus more
  water for cooking
½ onion
1 carrot
2 bay leaves
½ tsp sea salt

Start by removing any stones and dried-up discolored
beans. Place the dried beans and water in a container
and leave to soak for 6–8 hours (or overnight). Drain
and rinse the beans and place in a thick-bottomed
saucepan with a lid. Add over water until it is about
1 in above the beans, then add the onion, carrot and
bay leaves.

Bring to a boil then reduce the heat and simmer,
covered, until tender. This will take approximately
45–90 minutes, depending on the variety of beans.
Add salt when the beans are just tender. They are
done to perfection when you can mash one between
two fingers or with a fork. Drain off the liquid.

Store cooked beans in the fridge where they will keep,
covered, for 4–5 days.

BASIC METHODS

RAW DATE SYRUP
Makes about 2 cups

6 oz/1 cup medjool dates, pitted
1 tbsp freshly squeezed lemon juice
a pinch of sea salt

Place 1⅓ cups water, dates, lemon juice and salt in a high-speed blender or food processor. If you are using a food processor, start with a little less water and add gradually.
Run until you have a smooth syrup. Use instead of honey, agave or maple syrup. Keep in an airtight container in the fridge for a couple of weeks.

APPLE SYRUP
Makes about 1 cup

2.2 lbs apples
or
3 cups unfiltered apple juice

Start by juicing the whole apples in a juicer. Place the apple juice in heavy saucepan over high heat. Bring to a boil, lower the heat to medium and simmer for 45–60 minutes, stirring occasionally.
The apple juice will cook down to about one-third of its original volume and form apple syrup. Leave to cool slightly before pouring into an airtight container. Keeps in the fridge for up to one month.

Tip: You can flavor the syrup by adding spices during cooking. Star anise, clove, cinnamon, vanilla, saffron, ginger or cardamom are all delicious with this intense and sweet apple taste.

APPLE KETCHUP
Makes about 2½ cups

2 tbsp olive oil
2 green onions (scallions), finely chopped
2¼ lbs ripe tomatoes, diced
   (about 10 large)
1 small red apple, diced
3 tbsp apple cider vinegar
4 tbsp raisins
1 small banana, sliced
1 tbsp tomato paste
¼ tsp sweet paprika
1 tsp whole cloves
1 cinnamon stick
3 bay leaves
sea salt
freshly ground black pepper

Heat the oil and sauté the onions on medium-low heat in a heavy saucepan until soft, but not brown. Then add the rest of the ingredients and bring to a boil; lower the heat and let gently simmer for 40 minutes.
Remove the cloves, cinnamon and bay leaves. Taste and adjust the seasoning if necessary. Purée the ketchup with a hand (immersion) blender or leave it chunky if you prefer. Rinse a glass jar in boiling water. Pour the ketchup into the jar while it is still warm and seal immediately. Store in the fridge for up to 2 weeks.

Mornings

One of the things we love most about our apartment is the high ceiling and large windows. They give that feeling of space that is very rare to find in an urban apartment. The only time we don't love our windows is in the mornings. The sun sneaks in way too early during the summer and, like clockwork, I feel Elsa kicking at my ribs: *"Mor, mor vakna, jag vill spise frukost!"* ("Wake up Mommy, I want breakfast!"). Obviously, we are not morning people. But having a little morning person to feed every day has given us a new appreciation for the morning meal.

Elsa pulls us out of bed and into the kitchen right after she wakes up. And since we had her, we have actually started to eat breakfast together. Before that, David had a coffee on his way to work and I took a smoothie with me to the gym. Now we sit there, around the breakfast table, eating together and talking. Two hours ahead of schedule.

With all that time in the morning, we now have much more varied breakfasts. We often make porridge, but some days we have fruit salad, and other days a slice of cheese on thin crispbread. We still make smoothies, but nowadays we eat them from a bowl, topped with granola. All of these breakfasts are included in this chapter, along with many more. Some of them can be whipped up in five minutes (like Thin Omelet Rolls, page 54), while others take a little longer (like Dark Danish Rye Bread, page 58). Hopefully, you will be able to find something that fits into your morning schedule, too.

– Luise

Baked Crunchy Blackberry Oatmeal

14 oz/3¼ cups fresh blackberries (thawed if using frozen)
2 cups rolled oats
1 tsp baking powder
½ tsp ground ginger or 1 tsp grated fresh ginger
a pinch of sea salt
2 large eggs
2¼ cups almond milk (or milk of choice)

1 tsp pure vanilla extract
¼ cup pure unsweetened apple syrup (page 30), or honey, maple syrup or agave syrup
1 tbsp coconut oil (at room temperature), plus extra for greasing the pan
¾ cup pumpkin seeds (pepitas)
generous ½ cup hazelnuts, toasted

Serves 4–6

This is a typical Sunday morning recipe for us. We take turns on who gets to stay in bed, while the other gets up with Elsa to prepare this porridge and put it in the oven. And then we all jump back into the bed, and Elsa watches a cartoon while we slumber. Half an hour later, a wonderful scent of vanilla and nuts has filled the apartment, and we are ready to get up. The taste and texture is actually a combination of baked oatmeal and fruit crumble.

Preheat the oven to 375°F. Grease the bottom of an 8 x 10 in baking dish with coconut oil and spread the berries in an even layer in the dish, then set aside.

Combine the rolled oats, baking powder, ginger and salt in a mixing bowl. In a separate bowl, beat the eggs, add the milk and vanilla and whisk well to combine.

To create the crunchy top layer, put the apple syrup, 1 tbsp coconut oil, pumpkin seeds and hazelnuts in a small bowl and mix with your fingers to make sure everything is well coated.

Spoon the oat mixture into the baking dish to cover the blackberries, and then pour the egg mixture over the oats so everything is evenly soaked. Sprinkle the seed and nut mixture on top and bake for 35–40 minutes. When it's done, the oatmeal should be set and the nuts and seeds lightly browned and crunchy. Leave to cool slightly before serving.

Tip: For a vegan alternative: measure 2 tbsp chia seeds into a small bowl and add ⅓ cup water. Stir with a spoon and place in the fridge for 15 minutes. Use in place of the eggs.

Tip: For a gluten-free alternative, choose gluten-free oats.

Herb & Asparagus Frittata

8 large eggs, whisked
1 cup oat milk (page 27), or
  milk of choice
4 tbsp basil pesto, divided
½ tsp sea salt
2 tbsp olive oil, coconut oil
  or ghee (see page 25)
2 green onions, finely chopped
4 small potatoes (or 1 small sweet
  potato), thinly sliced
¾ cup shredded cabbage
3 fresh asparagus spears, shaved
  into ribbons with a potato peeler

Serves 4

If you peek in through our kitchen window on a random weekday morning you may well be watching us cooking an omelette or a frittata! It's part of our weekly repertoire. Our frittatas rarely look the same; we use whatever leftover vegetables we have in the fridge. This version is great when you have a few stalks of asparagus and some pesto. Shave the asparagus thinly and arrange on top of the frittata after it has baked or just towards the end of the baking time.

Preheat the oven to 400°F.

In a medium-size mixing bowl, whisk together the eggs, milk, 2 tbsp pesto and salt. Set aside.

Heat the olive oil in an 8 in ovenproof frying pan on medium heat. Add the onions, potato slices and cabbage. Stir with a spatula to make sure everything gets evenly fried. After about 5 minutes, when the vegetables are lightly golden and tender, remove to a plate and set aside.

Add a little extra oil to the pan, then pour in the egg mixture. Leave for about a minute, and then scatter the vegetables evenly on top of the egg. They will sink down into the mixture, but this way they won't get burned on the bottom. Cook for a minute, while carefully loosening the edges and bottom with a spatula. Transfer the pan to the oven and cook for about one minute, or until the frittata is golden brown on top and just cooked through in the middle. Remove from the oven, drizzle over the remaining pesto, top with the asparagus ribbons and serve.

Stone Fruit Salad with Creamy Goat Cheese

Serves 4

20 cherries, pitted and halved,
  plus a few whole to decorate
6 apricots, halved, pitted
  and sliced
2 saturn (flat) peaches, halved, pitted
  and sliced
2 peaches, halved, pitted
  and sliced
4 small plums, halved and pitted
1 handful of red currants or white
  currants
¼ cup Elderflower Lemonade (page 203)
  or unsweetened apple juice
scant ½ cup, soft, fresh goat cheese,
  crumbled

After a trip to Barcelona a few years ago, we came home with three large bags of fruit, vegetables and cheese from the market La Boqueria. We worked our way through everything but a bag of stone fruit and a big chunk of goat cheese. So we turned them into a salad. It was a completely unplanned combination and it tasted so good. You can have this dish for breakfast, but it is also nice as dessert or a lunch if you add some arugula leaves and more vegetables.

Combine all the fruit in a mixing bowl. Drizzle with elderflower lemonade and toss until all the fruit is coated. Leave for 15 minutes for the fruits to release their juices. Transfer to a serving plate and sprinkle with the crumbled goat cheese. Decorate with a few whole cherries or fresh elderflowers, if available.

Flour-free Banana & Coconut Pancakes

3 ripe bananas
6 large eggs, lightly beaten
½ cup shredded dried coconut,
   plus extra for sprinkling
1 cup blueberries (fresh or thawed
   if frozen)
½ tsp ground cinnamon
2 tsp coconut oil, for frying
2 tbsp maple syrup or plain
   yogurt, for topping (optional)

Makes 10 pancakes

These pancakes are nothing less than a family classic. We always prepare a large stack of them when we make brunch. We have been making them for years and have shared the recipe with most of our relatives and friends. And from what we have heard, they have passed the recipe on to their friends. The pancakes have a lovely fruity flavor and are easy and quick to make. What is also great is that they only call for a few ingredients, are completely flour-free and still very thick and rich. They also make a quick snack any time of day, and a perfect post-workout meal.

Mash the bananas with a fork in a medium-sized bowl. Add the eggs and coconut and whisk to blend. Add the blueberries (reserve a few for serving) and cinnamon and stir well.

Heat the coconut oil in a 10 in nonstick frying pan over medium heat. Add 2 to 3 tablespoons of batter for each pancake. You should be able to cook 3 to 4 pancakes in the pan at a time. Use a spatula to carefully flip the pancakes when they have set and the bottom is golden – about 2 minutes on the first side and 1 minute on the other.

Stack the pancakes and top with the reserved blueberries. On weekends we like to drizzle ours with maple syrup or yogurt and sprinkle with a little extra coconut.

Breakfast Blend

2 large apples, juiced, or 1 cup
  unsweetened apple juice
juice of 1 lemon
1 avocado, pitted and peeled
10 brazil nuts, soaked in cold water
  for 2–6 hours
1 handful of sprouted mung beans
  (see page 28, or use store-bought
½ in piece fresh ginger, grated
1 tbsp dried nettles
4 mint leaves
a couple of ice cubes

Serves 2

*This is a blend that we sometimes
make as an alternative to yogurt and
top with either fruit or granola. It
is actually just like a smoothie, but
we like to serve it in bowls instead
of glasses for breakfast. Not only is it
delicious, but also very rich in proteins
and minerals thanks to the nuts and
sprouted mung beans.*

Juice the apples and lemon in a juicer. Alternatively, use apple juice
and squeeze the lemon by hand. Pour the juice into a blender and add
the rest of the ingredients. Purée on high speed until smooth. Serve in
bowls and top with nuts, fruits, sprouts or granola.

Tip: For extra power, add wheatgrass, spirulina, hemp, protein powder,
bee pollen, rosehip powder or aloe vera.

Swedish Crispbread

1 cup lukewarm water
2 tsp sea salt
3 tsp active dry yeast
2 tbsp cumin seeds, divided
½ cup cultured buttermilk,
 filmjölk or kefir

1²/₃ cups whole-grain rye flour
1½ cups whole-grain spelt flour
¼ cup flax seeds, crushed (use a mortar
 and pestle or buy pre-crushed)
2 tbsp coarse sea salt

Makes 12 breads

You won't find a Scandinavian family that doesn't have crispbread at home. It's how we are raised. If you haven't tried it before, don't expect a bread; it's more like a cracker. When baking this, we can't emphasize enough the importance of making it thin. The thinner you make it, the crispier it becomes. It tastes fantastic with a nice cheese, thin slices of cucumber and some freshly ground black pepper. Crispbread is famous for keeping for several months when stored in an airtight container, but we usually finish a batch within a week!

Pour the lukewarm water into a medium-sized bowl. Add the salt, yeast and 1 tablespoon of the cumin seeds and stir with a wooden spoon. Stir in the buttermilk.

In a separate bowl, sift the rye flour and spelt flour together and add half of it to the yeast mixture. Gradually add more flour until the dough comes together enough for you to start kneading it. Knead for a couple of minutes in the bowl, adding more flour if it sticks to your hands. Divide the dough into 12 small buns, around 2 in wide, and place on a floured surface. Cover with a damp cloth and leave to rest for 1 hour.

Preheat the oven to 400°F. Place one of the buns on a sheet of parchment paper and use a rolling pin to roll it into a very thin disc, with a diameter of about 8 in. Cut a small hole out of the center of each to ensure even crispness. Sprinkle with some of the remaining 1 tbsp cumin seeds, and some of the crushed flax seeds and coarse sea salt. Prick each disc with a fork all over, then transfer to a baking sheet. Depending on the size of your oven, you can fit one or two breads on each baking sheet. Bake for around 8 minutes, until crisp and brown. Continue to roll out the rest of the buns, but always keep one eye on those in the oven. They are so thin that they go from baked to burned in no time. Cool on a wire rack.

Flowered Granola

BASIC INGREDIENTS
2 cups rolled oats
2 cups rolled rye or rolled spelt
1 cup nuts (such as almonds, hazelnuts or walnuts), coarsely chopped
¾ cup coconut flakes
scant 1 cup seeds (such as sunflower and pumpkin)
1 tsp ground spices (such as cardamom, nutmeg, clove or cinnamon)

LIQUIDS FOR ROASTING
4 tbsp liquid sweetener (such as apple syrup, honey, agave syrup or maple syrup)
4 tbsp coconut oil, melted (or water)

DRIED SUPERFOOD
½ cup mix of dried Nordic superberries (cranberries, rosehips, black currants, red currants, sea-buckthorn or elderberry), unsweetened
¼ cup edible organic dried flowers (or use a flower blend for herbal tea)

Makes about 3 pts/6 cups

We prefer to keep our granola simple – a few basic ingredients, some dried fruit and a natural sweetener. We usually add more spices during the winter and fewer in the summer. Use this recipe as a base, and then add your own favorite fruit, seeds and spices. We often prepare a batch of granola to give as gifts for Christmas and housewarming parties. Just wrap it in a nice old jar or paper bag with a homemade label.

Preheat the oven to 350°F. Line a baking sheet with parchment paper. Combine all the basic ingredients in a large bowl. Pour the liquid ingredients over and use your hands to toss until everything is well mixed and the dry ingredients are coated. Spread the granola mixture on the prepared baking sheet and roast in the oven for 15–20 minutes. Stir with a wooden spoon a couple of times during roasting to prevent burning.

Remove from the oven and leave to cool before adding the dried superfood. Add some extra spices if needed. Store the granola in a sealed glass jar at room temperature. Keeps for at least a month.

Thin Omelet Rolls with Apple & Cottage Cheese

OMELET
- 1 large egg
- 1 tbsp almond milk (or milk of choice)
- a pinch of sea salt
- 1 tsp ghee (see page 25), coconut oil or olive oil for frying

FILLING
- ½ red apple, cored and coarsely grated
- 3 tbsp plain cottage cheese
- a pinch of ground cinnamon
- 1 tbsp pumpkin seeds
- a few sprigs of thyme, leaves picked (optional)

Serves 1

Although Elsa eats almost anything we put in front of her, pancakes have always been a favorite. When we have time we make a large batch of Banana and Coconut Pancakes (on page 45) for all of us, but when we are in a hurry we make these. It is actually a thin omelet, but Elsa calls it a pancake. What is so great is that you don't have to make a whole batch. This recipe is for a single serving, but you could of course make more.

Whisk the egg, milk and a pinch of salt rapidly with a fork in a small bowl. Heat the ghee or oil in an 8 in nonstick frying pan over medium-high heat. Add the egg mixture and fry for
1 minute on the first side and 30–45 seconds on the other. Use a spatula to carefully flip the omelet.

Combine the filling in a small bowl. Place the omelet on a plate, spoon the filling in the middle and roll it up. Cut in half before serving. Also makes a good breakfast on the run, if wrapped in sandwich paper.

Buckwheat & Ginger Porridge

1¼ cups hulled whole buckwheat
⅓ cup dried fruit (prunes, apricots, cranberries, pear or whatever you have at home, coarsely chopped if large)
1 tbsp grated fresh ginger
2-3 cinnamon sticks
1 tsp cardamom seeds
½ tsp vanilla extract
a tiny pinch of sea salt
fresh blueberries and inca berries, to serve

Serves 4

Scandinavia has a long porridge tradition. In Copenhagen they even have a café devoted exclusively to grød (porridge). So it might not come as a surprise that we love porridge in our family. David's Mum taught us this recipe and it has become my absolute favorite porridge. It has a fantastic texture from the whole buckwheat; it's crumbly yet soft. And it is gluten-free. We sprinkle generous amounts of grated ginger over it before serving, but that is, of course, optional. Top it with seasonal fresh fruit or the Fig, Rhubarb and Pear Compote on page 160.
– Luise

Rinse the buckwheat in water, then add it to a medium saucepan together with 2½ cups water, the dried fruit, spices, vanilla and sea salt. Bring to a boil and lower the heat. Gently simmer for about 20 minutes, stirring occasionally.

When the water is absorbed, the porridge should be just about ready, but keep stirring for a few more minutes to get a crumbly texture. Remove the cinnamon sticks and serve in bowls with fresh fruit, grated ginger and oat milk.

Tip: Rinse the cinnamon sticks in cold water and re-use them.

Dark
Danish
Rye Bread

1 cup whole rye grains
½ cup sunflower seeds
2 cups boiling water
1 cup plain yogurt, at room temperature
3 tbsp honey
1 tbsp sea salt
1 tbsp fennel seeds

1 cup dried cranberries (optional)
5 tbsp carob powder (or cocoa powder)
4 tsp active dry yeast
2⅔ cups whole rye flour
1 cup whole spelt flour
½ cup light spelt flour

Makes 1 loaf

We knew from the minute we started testing recipes for this book that we wanted to include Danish rye bread. Like all Danish families, we often have a dark loaf at home. We have experimented with at least ten different ways of making this quicker, but it always affects the quality and flavor. Baking Danish rye bread is, and will always be, a 24-hour project. But it is worth it. It is full of flavor, has a fantastic, thick but moist texture, and keeps you nourished for hours. Top it with our Crunchy Curried Egg Salad (on page 178) and you have yourself a classic Danish smørrebrød.

Place the rye grains and sunflower seeds in a bowl and cover with the boiling water. Let sit for 15 minutes, then add the yogurt, honey, sea salt, fennel seeds, cranberries and carob powder and stir with a wooden spoon. Use your finger to test the temperature of the mixture – it should be just warm.

Stir in the yeast. Then add rye flour and stir until you have a smooth batter. Cover the bowl with plastic wrap and leave for 1 hour at room temperature, until the dough is slightly bubbly. Mix together the spelt flours. Gradually add in enough of the spelt flour to form a dough. Turn out onto a floured work surface. Knead for about 5 minutes, adding the remaining spelt flour until it is firmer, but still slightly sticky and quite heavy. Form it into a ball and return to the bowl. Slap some water on the top with your hands. Cover with plastic wrap and chill for 8–10 hours, or overnight.

Place the dough into a 9 x 5 in oiled loaf pan and press down with your fists to get rid of any air pockets. The dough should be quite sticky. Brush the top with water and dust it with rye flour. Cover with a kitchen towel and set aside to rise slightly for 2 hours.

Preheat the oven to 400°F. Bake the loaf on the lowest shelf for 1 hour. Turn off the heat and leave the loaf in the oven for an additional 15 minutes. Remove from the pan and leave to cool on an wire rack for at least 4 hours. This is important to allow the bread to set, which makes it easier to cut. Keep for about one week.

Lighter Meals

Every Friday we have a delivery of locally harvested seasonal vegetables and fruit. Although we never know exactly what will arrive in each box, we can expect fresh asparagus in April, gooseberries in July and tomatoes in August. It's our way of keeping it seasonal even though we live in a city apartment, far from crops, fruit trees and tractors. The small, shiny apples, with the blossoms and half of the branch still on, will probably be eaten up in an instant. Apart from those, we usually save most of the contents until after the weekend because it is usually during the weekdays that we use them the most.

We prefer our weekday meals to be light, and if they are quick to make, we love them even more. One of the simplest and best ways of using the flavorful and crispy fresh vegetables and fruit is to add them to a salad, together with a handful of toasted seeds, some sprouted lentils and perhaps also a slice of goat cheese. That's perfect for us. It could be our Tuesday lunch as well as our Thursday dinner (for dinner we would probably add some Dijon and lemon marinated quinoa). Simple food that allows the ingredients to shine – this is the kind of food you will find in this chapter. Salads, a few soups, a fresh nettle pesto, a pizza crust made with cauliflower and our own version of tacos (wrapped in savoy cabbage leaves).

Baked Herb & Pistachio Falafel

FALAFELS
- 8 sprigs of mint, leaves picked
- 8 sprigs of parsley, leaves picked
- 8½ oz/generous 2 cups shelled pistachio nuts
- 12 oz/2 cups chickpeas (garbanzo beans), cooked or canned
- 2 garlic cloves
- ½ small onion
- 3 tbsp extra virgin olive oil
- 1 tsp ground cumin
- 1 tbsp buckwheat flour (or another gluten-free flour)
- 1 tsp baking soda

CASHEW NUT DRESSING
- 6 tbsp cashew butter or other Nut Butter (see page 27)
- 6 tbsp canola oil
- 3 tbsp freshly squeezed lemon juice
- a pinch of sea salt

TOMATO CHILI SALSA
- 3 tomatoes, diced
- ½ small fresh red chili, seeded and finely chopped
- 1 garlic clove, finely chopped
- 3 tbsp extra virgin olive oil
- 2 tsp chopped oregano
- sea salt and freshly ground black pepper

Makes about 24 falafels

We love falafel, but we do not understand why it is always made into greasy, deep-fried fast food. Although fast food can be nice at times, we mostly prefer our meals on the lighter side. So we decided to make our own version and change some essential details. First of all, we pack it with fresh spices and pistachio nuts, which give it a wonderful color, flavor and texture. We have never been fans of deep-frying and therefore we oven-bake our falafels. Lastly, we wrap them up in thin and crispy cabbage leaves instead of pita bread. Try it—we promise that you have never had a falafel that makes you feel so good afterwards.

TO SERVE
- 1 large white cabbage
- 1 cup Raita (see page 89)
- 1 handful of grapes, grapes halved
- ⅓ cup sunflower seeds, toasted
- 1 handful of fresh herbs, leaves picked

FOR THE FALAFELS
Preheat the oven to 375°F.

Blend the herbs in a food processor for about 30 seconds. Add the pistachio nuts and pulse until well combined. Add the remaining falafel ingredients to the food processor and blend for about a minute, stopping and scraping down the sides as necessary. Try to keep the texture of the falafel paste a little rough.

Remove the paste and, using your hands, form 24 small round falafels. Place on a baking sheet lined with parchment paper and bake for about 15 minutes. Turn them every 5 minutes to evenly brown.

FOR THE CASHEW NUT DRESSING
Whisk all the ingredients together in a small bowl until they are combined.

FOR THE TOMATO CHILI SALSA
Combine all the ingredients in a bowl and stir to combine. Season to taste with salt and pepper. Refrigerate for 30 minutes to intensify the flavors.

ASSEMBLY
Turn the cabbage upside down and remove the cone with a sharp knife. Rinse it under cold running water and gently separate the large outer leaves one by one. Pat them dry with paper towels. Place all the accompaniments in small bowls and place on the table so everyone can assemble their own falafel.

Tom Kha Tofu

4 kaffir lime leaves
2 tbsp extra virgin olive oil (in Thailand they mix a bit of sweet chili paste in the oil, to get the red color)
1 small fresh red chili, seeded and finely chopped
16 cilantro leaves
8 cherry tomatoes, halved
4 stalks of lemongrass
4 in piece galangal (or fresh ginger), peeled and coarsely chopped

4¼ cups coconut milk
2 handfuls of oyster mushrooms (or cremini mushrooms), halved
2 cups sliced white cabbage
12 oz block firm tofu, cut in quarters
juice of 2 limes
a pinch of sea salt
a few cilantro leaves, to serve

Serves 4

When Elsa was six months old we travelled around the world together. We spent two months in Thailand and Tom Kha Tofu became one of our favorite meals. It is basically a mild coconut milk soup with a lime flavor, filled with mushrooms, tofu, cabbage and tomato. We got to know the chef at a lovely little restaurant, and luckily she was happy to share the recipe with us. The kha root, also known as galangal or blue ginger, is authentic in this dish. It's available from Asian stores or larger supermarkets, or use fresh ginger instead.

Remove the thick rib from the kaffir lime leaves, roll them up tight and chop them very finely.

Divide the oil, chili, cilantro and tomatoes among 4 serving bowls and set aside. Crush the lemongrass and galangal, using the back of a knife, and put them in a large saucepan together with the coconut milk. Bring to a boil, then lower the heat and add the chopped kaffir lime leaves, mushrooms, cabbage, tofu, lime juice and salt. Let it gently simmer on low heat for 3–4 minutes. Taste and add more salt if needed.

Pour the soup over the tomatoes and spices in the bowls, garnish with fresh cilantro and serve.

LIGHTER MEALS

Broccoli Salad with Pomegranate & Raisins

2 heads of fresh broccoli
1 small red onion, finely chopped
seeds from 1 pomegranate
1¼ cups raisins
generous ½ cup sunflower seeds,
    toasted
1 cup plain yogurt
½ tsp sea salt
freshly ground black pepper

Serves 4

This is a wonderful quick salad that has a nice crunchy texture and fresh flavors. Sweet raisins and fresh pomegranate meet raw broccoli, coated in a tangy yogurt dressing. It makes a great side dish or light lunch with a slice of toasted rye bread.

Separate the broccoli florets from the stalks and cut them into smaller, bite-sized pieces. Cut the stalks in half lengthwise and finely slice. Place in a serving bowl, together with the onion, pomegranate seeds, raisins and sunflower seeds. Toss to combine. Add the yogurt, salt, and pepper, to taste. Use your hands to mix together making sure that all broccoli florets are coated in yogurt. Serve.

Tip: The traditional way to make this salad is with mayonnaise. Our version is lighter but you could use mayonnaise instead or use half of each.

Tip: For a vegan alternative, use soy yogurt.

Quinoa & Cauliflower Cakes with Ramps

1 cup white quinoa
1⅔ cups cauliflower florets
1 large handful wild garlic or ramps,
  coarsely chopped
4 large eggs
1⅓ cups crumbled feta cheese
¾ cup rolled oats
sea salt and freshly ground black pepper
2 tbsp Ghee (see page 25), coconut oil
  or olive oil, for frying

Makes 12 cakes

*We often take whatever leftovers
we have, scrape them together with
some goat or sheep's milk cheese,
and fry them into small cakes that
we eat with a salad or a coleslaw.
It's often quinoa, but sometimes also
millet, buckwheat or oats. During the
spring we always get fresh bundles of
wild ramps from David's mom and
that is our favorite way to flavor
these cakes. If you cannot find ramps,
use fresh spinach and add two cloves
of crushed garlic.*

Cook the quinoa: Combine 2¼ cups water, the quinoa and a pinch of salt in a medium-sized saucepan. Bring to a boil, reduce the heat and gently simmer for about 15 minutes, or until you see small tails on the quinoa seeds. Drain any excess water and set aside to cool.

Place the cauliflower in a food processor and pulse until it is a rice-like texture. Transfer to a bowl and add the quinoa, ramps, eggs, feta, oats, and salt and pepper. Stir until well combined. Place in the fridge to set for 30 minutes.

Form the mixture into 12 patties with your hands. Heat the ghee or oil in a large frying pan on medium-high heat. Add 4 patties at a time and fry for about 3–4 minutes, or until golden brown. Flip carefully and fry the other side for 2–3 minutes more. Continue until all the patties are fried. Drain on paper towels.

These are delicious served warm or cold.

Tip: For a gluten-free alternative, choose gluten-free rolled oats.

LIGHTER MEALS

Wild Nettle Pesto

5–7 oz young nettle leaves
1 large handful of basil leaves
1–2 garlic cloves, according to taste
juice of ½ lemon
⅓ cup extra virgin olive oil
¼ cup pine nuts, lightly toasted
¼ cup grated Pecorino Romano cheese

Makes about ½ cup

*Even though we – out of stupidity –
tried this recipe using nettles that grow
in the park just around the corner
from our apartment, we wouldn't
recommend using city nettles. We
learned afterwards that these little
stingers actually live on nitrogen, and
absorb all the bad stuff that floats
around in a city. But if you are in
the countryside during spring, pick
the tops off young nettle plants. They
are packed with iron and, as well as
making this pesto, you can also make
soup or add them to the Quinoa and
Cauliflower Cakes with Ramps on
page 71. When crushed or mixed
they lose their sting, but don't forget
to wear gloves when picking them.
We love this pesto with whole-grain
pasta, but it also makes a great spread
for bread or a dipping sauce for raw
vegetables.*

Add half of the olive oil and all of the other ingredients to a mortar,
blender or a food processor. Pound or blend, while gradually adding
the remaining oil, until everything is combined and is a glistening paste.
Taste and add more oil, lemon juice, salt or pepper if required.

Wild Rice, Sunchoke & Grape Salad

10 sunchokes (Jerusalem artichokes)
2 tbsp extra virgin olive oil
salt and freshly ground black pepper
2 sprigs of thyme, leaves picked
generous 1 cup wild rice, rinsed
20 red grapes, halved and seeded,
　if necessary
2 cups shredded red cabbage
1 handful of watercress, mâche,
　or arugula

DRESSING
　¼ cup extra virgin olive oil
　juice and zest of 1 small orange
　2 sprigs of thyme, leaves picked
　salt and freshly ground black pepper

Serves 4

This is one of the prettiest salads we know. It is quite simple, but it could easily be served at a fancy dinner party. With an elegant meal, it would be a good idea to sprout the rice instead of cooking it, which makes it even prettier and more nutritious. This salad combines earthy wild rice flavors with sweetness from the roasted sunchokes and fresh grapes.

Preheat the oven to 400°F.

Scrub the sunchokes and cut them into ½ in slices. Place them on a baking sheet, drizzle immediately with the olive oil, and sprinkle with sea salt, pepper and fresh thyme. Roast in the oven for about 45 minutes or until soft in the middle and golden and slightly crispy on the outside. Meanwhile, prepare the rice. Bring 3 cups water to a boil, add the wild rice and a teaspoon of salt. Reduce the heat and let it gently simmer, covered, for 40 minutes or just until the kernels puff open. Drain off any excess water.

Whisk the dressing ingredients together in a bowl and set aside. Place sunchokes and rice in a large bowl. Add the grapes, cabbage and dressing and toss lightly, using your hands, so all ingredients are coated. Garnish with sprigs of watercress and serve warm or cold.

LIGHTER MEALS

Roasted Tomato & Chickpea Soup

2 lb 3 oz ripe tomatoes, halved
2⅔ cups cooked chickpeas (garbanzos)
4 sprigs of oregano, leaves picked
1 tsp paprika
6 garlic cloves, crushed with the back
  of a knife
2 tbsp extra virgin olive oil
sea salt
plain yogurt and a few oregano leaves,
  to garnish

Serves 2–4

*We often keep the most beautiful
tomatoes on our kitchen counter,
but forget to use them. They sit there
waiting patiently. You can almost see
how they start jumping for joy every
time our hands come close. Days pass,
and they turn riper and riper until
one day they are almost too ripe to use.
That is when we roast them and mix
them into this soup. It has a wonderful
roasted, mild flavor and a creamy
texture thanks to the chickpeas.
You can, of course, use fresh young
tomatoes instead, but we have found
that very ripe tomatoes have a more
intense, sweet flavor.*

Preheat the oven to 400°F.

Place the tomatoes, chickpeas, oregano, paprika and garlic on a
baking sheet. Drizzle with the olive oil, place in the oven and bake for
about an hour, or until the tomatoes are slightly blackened in places
and bubbling. Remove from the oven (save a few chickpeas for
serving), scrape all ingredients into a blender or food processor and
blend until smooth.

Add a little water if needed. Serve in bowls or glasses, with a dollop
of yogurt, fresh oregano leaves and a few roasted chickpeas on top.
This is delicious served with a slice of sourdough bread.

Savory Tacos with Corn & Mango Filling

CORN AND MANGO FILLING
- 2 ears of corn
- 2⅔ cups cooked black beans, drained (see tip)
- 1 small green onion, finely chopped
- 1 mango, peeled and sliced
- ½ cup dried coconut flakes
- grated zest and juice of 1 lime
- 1 tbsp extra virgin olive oil
- 1 tsp ground cumin
- 1 pinch each of cayenne pepper, paprika, and dried oregano
- sea salt

RAW CASHEW CREAM SAUCE
- 1 cup raw cashew nuts, soaked in cold water for at least 1 hour
- 1 tbsp apple cider vinegar
- juice of ½ lemon
- a pinch of sea salt

TO SERVE
- 1 savoy cabbage or collard greens
- 2 ripe avocados, pitted, peeled and sliced
- 1 large handful of cilantro, leaves picked and chopped

Serves 4

If we had to choose one dish that illustrates our style of cooking, this version of tacos would probably be a good candidate. They combine vegetables with fruit and beans, they are served in leaves rather than bread, and they look spectacularly beautiful. Not to mention that they're filled with a fiesta of fresh flavors!

FOR THE TACO FILLING

Use a sharp knife to cut off the corn kernels from all sides of the cobs and place them in a mixing bowl. Add the beans, green onion, mango, coconut flakes, lime zest and juice, olive oil and spices. Toss gently with your hands to make sure that everything is coated. Set aside.

FOR THE RAW CASHEW CREAM SAUCE

Add all the ingredients to a blender and purée until completely smooth. If you like it a bit runnier add some water. Pour the sauce into a bowl and chill in the fridge while you prepare the cabbage.

ASSEMBLY

Turn the cabbage upside down and remove the cone by cutting around it with a sharp knife. Rinse it under cold running water and gently separate the leaves one by one. Pat them dry with paper towels. Remove the middle rib in each leaf with a sharp knife and cut each leaf in half. Place the leaves on a work surface, put a spoonful of filling onto each leaf, followed by a little raw sour cream sauce and a few avocado slices. Top with some chopped cilantro before folding over the cabbage leaf and securing with a toothpick. Alternatively, place all the taco components on the table and let people help themselves.

Tip: If you prefer this dish raw, use sprouted beluga lentils instead of cooked black beans in the filling.

Lemony Fennel & Lentil Salad

FOR THE MARINADE
- juice of 1 large lemon
- 2 tbsp honey
- sea salt
- freshly ground black pepper

FOR THE SALAD
- 1 fennel bulb and leaves (they look like dill), sliced paper-thin
- 4 large handfuls of crisp lettuce
- 1 cucumber, peeled, seeded and sliced
- 1 cup green lentils, sprouted (see page 28) or cooked
- 7 oz creamy ash-coated goat cheese roll, cut into ½ in slices

Serves 4

I think both David and I were served too much lettuce when we were kids. For a long time we rarely felt like making anything with it, even if we had a whole head in our fridge. Most of the time, it just went straight to the compost. I know now what a waste that was. Fresh crisp lettuce has both character and a nice texture; it just needs to be paired with the right things. This is the salad that helped us appreciate it again. Crisp lettuce is topped with thin slices of lemon-marinated fennel, protein-rich green lentils, locally grown cucumber and thick slices of ashed goat cheese. Serve it on its own or as a side dish at a barbecue gathering.
– Luise

Whisk the marinade ingredients together in a small bowl. Place the slices of fennel in a shallow dish then pour the marinade over. Toss with your hands so that all slices are coated. Set aside for 10 minutes. Put the lettuce in a large bowl, add the cucumber and lentils, then add the marinated fennel together with the juices and toss to combine. Tuck in slices of goat cheese and serve.

Pizza with a Cauliflower Crust

florets from 1 head of cauliflower
¾ cup ground almonds
1 tbsp dried oregano
sea salt and freshly ground black
 pepper
3 large eggs, beaten

Makes 1 pizza

This recipe is for a healthier pizza crust. Cauliflower instead of flour – crazy, right? It is, in fact, super tasty and really quick to make. No leavening needed, just mix it up and bake. You can find several topping suggestions on pages 142–143, or use any of your own favorites.

Preheat the oven to 400°F and line a baking sheet with parchment paper. Coarsely chop the cauliflower, place in a food processor and blend until it is a fine rice-like texture. Measure 3 cups of the cauliflower "rice" and place in a mixing bowl. Add the ground almonds, oregano and salt and pepper and mix with your hands. Make a well in the center and add the eggs. Use your hands to pull the dry ingredients towards the middle until everything is combined and you can shape it into a ball. It should be more loose and sticky than traditional pizza dough.

Transfer to the parchment-lined baking sheet and form into a pizza base by flattening the dough with your hands. Make the edges slightly higher. Bake for about 25–30 minutes, or until golden.

Meanwhile, prepare the pizza toppings of your choice (see pages 142–143 for topping recipes). Remove the pizza from the oven. Cover it with the toppings and return to the oven for about 5–10 more minutes.

Tip: For a vegan alternative, replace the eggs with this chia mixture: Measure ¼ cup of chia seeds into a bowl and add ¾ cup water. Stir well and place in the fridge for 15 minutes before using.

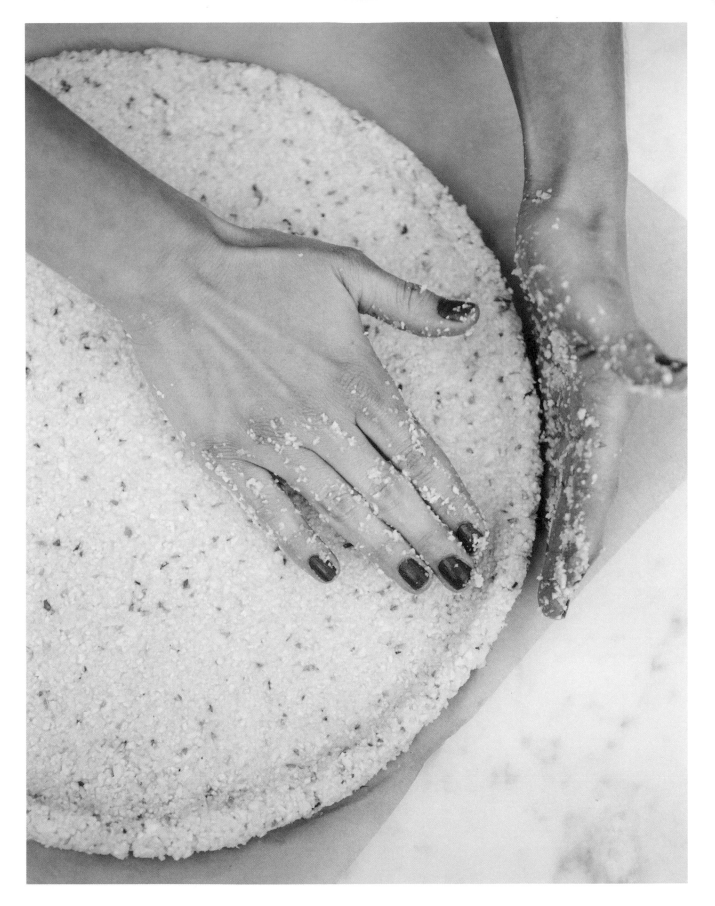

LIGHTER MEALS

Indian Chickpea Crêpes with Raita & Leafy Greens

Makes 12 cakes

Soft in the middle with crispy edges, these are the perfect crêpes – and yet they are made without any egg or milk. The secret ingredients are carbonated water and protein-rich chickpea flour, called besan flour, which you can find in Asian markets or health food stores. We have spiced them up with a host of Indian flavors.

RAITA

- 1 cup plain yogurt
- 1 cucumber, peeled, seeded and grated
- 4 large sprigs of mint, leaves picked and very finely chopped
- 1 in piece fresh green chili, seeded and very finely chopped
- 1 garlic clove, pressed
- 1 tsp cumin seeds

CHICKPEA CREPES

- 2 cups chickpea (garbanzo) flour
- ½ tsp ground turmeric
- ½ tsp ground cayenne pepper
- ½ tsp ground ginger
- ½ tsp curry powder
- ½ tsp ground coriander
- ½ tsp nigella seeds
- 1 tsp sea salt
- 2½ cups soda water
- Ghee (see page 25) or coconut oil, for frying
- 7 oz leafy greens, to serve

Start by preparing the raita. Place all the ingredients in a medium-sized bowl, stir together and chill in the fridge for at least 30 minutes before serving.

To make the crêpes, sift together the chickpea flour, spices and salt in a large bowl. Whisk in the soda water and chill the batter in the fridge for 30 minutes.

When you are ready to start cooking, heat the ghee in a large, nonstick frying pan over medium heat. Pour around ⅓ cup batter into the pan and give it a good swirl so that it spreads thinly across the entire pan. Wait until the base of the pancake is a deep golden color, then flip with a spatula and cook the other side until golden and cooked through. Repeat until you have used up all the batter.

Serve the crêpes warm with leafy greens and the raita. Also delicious served alongside a stew, such as the Rhubarb, Apple & Yellow Split Pea Stew on page 116.

Tip: For a vegan alternative, use soy yogurt.

Good to Go

On sunny days we often pack some leftovers and a blanket in a basket and walk to a park just down from where we live. Stockholm is nice that way. There are parks, water and green areas in every part of the city. So even though we don't have a terrace, balcony or garden, we get to eat outside pretty often during the summer months.

We also go on more planned picnics. Elsa gets all giddy whenever we visit the city farm, which is only a bus ride away. We usually take some wraps or muffins to eat and she gives an apple to the horses. And we sometimes take a small ferry to Rosendals Trädgård, a lovely garden where you can eat a picnic under the blossoming apple trees in spring. When Elsa was three months old, we arranged a picnic there so all our relatives and friends could come and meet her. Everybody brought food, which we shared together under a large oak tree.

In this chapter we have listed some recipes that can survive a few hours in a picnic basket without looking sad. For example, our picnic bread roll, with vegetables hidden inside; a delicious cold potato salad and small fennel and coconut tarts. All these dishes would also be great to take to a gathering during the winter.

Savory Corn & Millet Muffins

⅔ cup raw millet
1 cup cornmeal
1 cup rice flour
2 tsp baking powder
1 tsp baking soda
1 tsp sea salt
3 large eggs, beaten

1 cup soy yogurt, or yogurt of choice
½ cup extra virgin olive oil
around 25 kalamata olives, pitted
  and halved
1⅓ cups crumbled feta cheese
3 sprigs of oregano, leaves picked

Makes 12 medium-sized muffins

Baking gluten-free bread can be a challenge for anyone, as it often requires special ingredients and many different flours. Gluten-free muffins, however, are a lot easier. We often bake a vegan version of these as a midday snack for Elsa's preschool. We use olives, but any savory filling will work just as well.

Preheat the oven to 350°F. Line a muffin pan with muffin liners. Cover the millet with ½ cup boiling water and let sit for 5 minutes, then rinse in cold water. This is to extract the bitter taste from the millet shell and to make it softer. Mix the millet with the cornmeal, rice flour, baking powder, baking soda and salt.

In another bowl, beat the eggs until fluffy. Add the yogurt and olive oil and stir together. Add to the dry ingredients and stir with a wooden spoon until everything is incorporated. Add the olives, feta cheese and oregano and stir well.

Spoon about two heaped spoonfuls into each muffin cup. Bake for about 20 minutes, rotating the tin halfway through to make sure the muffins are evenly cooked. They are ready when golden and crusty on top. Best served warm.

Tip: For a vegan alternative, omit the feta cheese and replace the eggs with chia seeds. Measure 3 tbsp chia seeds in a bowl and add scant 1 cup water. Stir well and place in the fridge for 15 minutes before using.

Fennel & Coconut Tart

TART SHELL
- generous ½ cup rice flour
- scant ⅓ cup almond flour (or chestnut flour)
- 2 tbsp potato flour, tapioca flour or cornstarch
- ½ tsp sea salt
- 3 tbsp coconut oil or ghee (see page 25)
- 3 tbsp ice-cold water

FENNEL FILLING
- ½ cup coconut milk
- 2 large eggs, beaten
- ½ tsp freshly grated nutmeg
- 2 sprigs of rosemary, leaves picked and chopped
- sea salt and freshly ground black pepper
- 1 fennel bulb, very thinly sliced

Makes 1 large 8 in tart or 4 small 4 in tarts

Fennel is a beautiful vegetable and we have often talked about how we can let it shine properly. Our Lemony Fennel and Lentil Salad on page 84 is one attempt, but I think this tart is an even better example. The sweet coconut filling enhances its characteristic anise-like flavor. No cheese is needed here! The gluten-free pastry shell is made with almond flour and has a sweet flavor and just the right texture.

To make the tart shell, sift together the flours and salt in a bowl. Add the coconut oil and ice-cold water and use your hands to work the dry ingredients towards the center until a dough forms. If it feels crumbly, add 1–2 tablespoons more water. Gather it into a ball, wrap in plastic wrap and chill for 30 minutes in the fridge.

Meanwhile, make the filling. Whisk the coconut milk, eggs, nutmeg, rosemary, salt and pepper together in a small bowl until combined. Preheat oven to 375°F.

Use your hands to press the dough evenly into the bottom and up the sides of the tart pan. If making four smaller tarts, divide the dough into four equal pieces before pressing into the pans. Trim the dough flush with edge of the pan and prick the base with a fork to prevent the pastry from rising as it bakes.

Pour coconut and egg mixture into the tart shell then place the fennel slices on top. Place in the middle of the oven and bake for about 35 minutes or until the tart is golden and crispy.

Tip: Make the dough a day ahead. Wrap tightly in plastic wrap and leave in the fridge until you're ready to use it.

GOOD TO GO

Beet, Apple & Goat Cheese Wraps

Makes 8 wraps

BEET FILLING
13 oz red beets (about 4–5 medium-sized)

10½ oz/1¼ cups soft fresh goat cheese

sea salt and freshly ground black pepper

ORANGE QUINOA FILLING
1 cup white quinoa, rinsed

1 tsp fennel seeds

a pinch of sea salt

finely grated zest and juice of ½ orange

generous ½ cup raisins

3½ oz/scant 1 cup toasted walnuts, chopped

8 whole-grain or corn tortillas or large collard green leaves

4 large spinach leaves (torn in two)

2 avocados, pitted, peeled and sliced

3 small eating apples, grated

Wraps are an ideal picnic food. They keep very well, you don't need cutlery, and they can be made in endless varieties. We usually like to combine a few different fillings in our wraps to make them more interesting to eat. Raw beets are a favorite of ours. They taste much fresher than cooked, especially when combined with apple and goat cheese. Raisins are added for sweetness and walnuts for crunch. Cooked lentils would also be a great addition.

To prepare the beet filling, peel the beets, cut into quarters and place in a blender or food processor, then pulse a few times to finely chop. Add the goat cheese and salt and pepper. Blend for about 30 seconds or until the mixture has the consistency of a rough-textured spread. Taste and add more salt or pepper if needed. If you don't have a blender or food processor, use a grater to shred the beets and use your hands to mix the grated beets and the crumbled goat cheese together.

For the quinoa filling bring 2¼ cups of water to a boil in a small pan. Add the quinoa, fennel seeds and salt and gently simmer for about 15–20 minutes, until tender and the liquid is absorbed. Set aside to cool. Add the orange zest and juice, raisins and walnuts and stir to combine.

ASSEMBLY

Put 2–3 spoonfuls of the beet filling in the middle of each tortilla (not all the way to the edge) and cover with half a spinach leaf. Place a couple of spoonfuls of the quinoa filling on top and finish with some slices of avocado and grated apple.

Fold the top and bottom edges over the filling. Roll the whole tortilla from left to right to wrap in the filling. Roll some parchment or waxed paper around them and tie with string to hold them together while you transport them. Done! Cut the wraps in half before serving.

GOOD TO GO

Apple & Mushroom-stuffed Picnic Bread Roll

1 tbsp active dry yeast
1 cup water, heated to about 100°F
1 tbsp honey
1 tbsp sea salt
1¾ cups light spelt flour
1½ cups whole spelt flour
2 tbsp extra virgin olive oil

FOR THE FILLING
3 tbsp extra virgin olive oil, divided
1 leek, white part only, sliced
1 garlic clove, minced
10 cremini (or button) mushrooms, quartered
1 green eating apple, peeled, cored and cut into ½ in pieces
juice of ½ lemon
2 oz/½ cup grated Pecorino Romano cheese
3 sprigs thyme, leaves picked
freshly ground black pepper

Makes about 10 portions

I first tried this brilliant bread while living in Italy. They typically make it for Easter, but I'd say it's even more perfect for summer picnics. Instead of putting toppings on baked bread, they are hidden inside before baking and as you break off the first piece, you discover the delicious filling. This is our suggestion for a savory filling, but you could make it into a dessert by adding extra sweetness to the dough and filling it with fruit, honey and mascarpone cheese.

Put the yeast in a large bowl, add the water, honey and salt and stir until dissolved. In a separate bowl, sift the flours together, and then add half to the yeast mixture. Stir with a wooden spoon before gradually adding the rest of the flour. Knead in the bowl for a minute, then knead on a floured surface for a few minutes more. Add more flour if it feels too sticky. You want the dough to be elastic but not sticking to your hands. Rub the olive oil over the dough and form it into a ball. Return it to the bowl, cover with plastic wrap and leave to rise for about 1 hour.

Meanwhile, prepare the vegetable filling. Pour 1 tbsp olive oil in a frying pan on medium heat. Add the leek and garlic and sauté for a few minutes. Add the mushrooms and apple and fry for 3–4 minutes, stirring regularly. Season with salt and pepper. Remove from the heat, squeeze over the lemon juice and leave to cool.

When the dough has risen, re-knead briefly on a floured surface. Place the dough on a sheet of parchment paper. Roll out a rectangle, around 12 x 16 in and around ½ in thick. Drizzle with the remaining olive oil. Spread the filling evenly on bottom half of the dough and sprinkle with the Pecorino. Top with the thyme and some pepper.

Use the parchment paper to roll the dough into a log. Brush one of the ends with water then form the dough into a ring. Pinch the two ends together to form a closed tube. Place on a baking sheet. Sprinkle with flour and leave to rise under a tea towel for 30 minutes.

Preheat the oven to 400°F. When the roll has risen, bake for about 35–40 minutes, or until golden. Serve warm or cold.

Potato Salad with Dill & Horseradish

2 lb 3 oz small new potatoes
15–20 small heirloom tomatoes, halved
7 oz/2 cups fresh sugarsnap peas, sliced
  lengthwise
1 large handful of fresh dill, coarsely
  chopped

DRESSING
  1 in piece fresh horseradish, grated
  2–3 tbsp apple cider vinegar
  2–3 tbsp extra virgin olive oil
  sea salt and freshly ground
    black pepper

Serves 4

Not only is this salad beautiful, with the multicolored heirloom tomatoes, sugarsnap peas, potatoes and dill scattered all over, it is also packed with flavor and acidity from freshly grated horseradish and apple cider vinegar. It's one of our favorite summer salads. We often have this as a side dish at barbecue parties.

Place the potatoes in a saucepan with just enough cold salted water to cover. Bring to a boil then reduce to simmer for 15 minutes. Test with a small sharp knife – when the potatoes fall off the knife they are done. Drain and set aside to cool.

Meanwhile combine the tomatoes, peas and dill in a large serving bowl. Whisk together the dressing ingredients in a small bowl. When the potatoes have cooled place them in the serving bowl, pour the dressing over and toss with your hands so everything is coated. Serve.

Maple-tossed Beluga Lentil Salad

1 cup beluga or Puy lentils
2 thin red rhubarb sticks,
  thinly sliced
20 strawberries, sliced
scant 1 cup shelled edamame beans
small handful of fresh red currants,
  optional
8 asparagus spears, cut into 1 in pieces
15 basil leaves

DRESSING
3 tbsp maple syrup
3 tbsp extra virgin olive oil
juice of ½ lemon
sea salt and freshly ground
  black pepper

Serves 4

This salad is a celebration of all the wonderful fruit and vegetables that are in season during the spring. Raw rhubarb is sliced thinly and tossed in a maple dressing, which adds both tartness and sweetness. Beluga lentils are great in picnic salads as they stay firm even after a bumpy car ride.

Rinse the lentils under running water. Transfer to a medium saucepan, together with 2¼ cups water and bring to a boil. Reduce the heat and gently simmer for about 15–20 minutes or until tender. When almost done, add a pinch of salt, then drain and set aside to cool.

Prepare all the salad ingredients and place in a large bowl, together with the cooled lentils. Whisk together the ingredients for the dressing, add to the salad and toss with your hands until everything is well coated. Top with a couple of basil leaves.

Divide between four small glass jars, cover with lids and you are ready to go. Serve with a piece of sourdough bread.

Tip: This is a vegan recipe, but you could crumble some feta cheese over the salads in each jar to make it even more nourishing.

Strawberry Gazpacho

1 lb 5 oz/4 cups fresh strawberries,
   hulled and halved
1 lb 2 oz watermelon, seeded and
   cut into 1 in chunks
1 red bell pepper, seeded
   and chopped
2 small green onions, halved
15 mint leaves
juice of ½ lemon
1 celery rib, chopped
4 drops of Tabasco (or more
   to taste)

Serves 4–6

*We love the concept of a chilled soup
and although we appreciate a classic
gazpacho, we often prefer to make this
slightly sweeter version. Instead of
tangy tomatoes, this soup oozes fruit.
We balance it with onion, celery, mint
and a few drops of Tabasco.*

Put all the ingredients in a blender or a food processor. Pulse until you
have a soup consistency, taste it and season with salt, pepper and more
lemon if needed. Store in a large bottle in the fridge. If you are taking
it to a picnic, put a few ice cubes in the bottle just before you leave so it
stays cool. Take along a few glasses for serving.

GOOD TO GO

Family Dinners

In our living room we have a very beautiful, big dinner table. I got it from my mother, and I think she got it from her father. It's a wooden table, probably more than a hundred years old, with scratches and marks from dinners in the past. We really love that table. Unfortunately I have a hunch that it doesn't love us back because we never eat on it. Sometimes we come there with a bowl full of food, only to take a photo for the blog. Or we use it to sort papers or put Elsa's toys on. I realize how insulting it must be for a table with that kind of history, but it is just how things have turned out. As much as I love that table, it is just easier eating in the kitchen, close to all our pots, pans, pepper and salt.

The only time we do use our dinner table is when we have friends or family over for a meal. Then we fill it with plates, cutlery and glasses (we never use a cloth, scratching the table has always been part of the deal). We dim the lights in our living room and put on a Nina Simone record. When, later during the night, I listen to the buzz as everyone is talking and eating, glasses clinking and chairs scraping the floor, I always think *we should do this more often*. And probably, so does our table.

The dinners in this chapter should be nourishing enough to satisfy both vegetarians and meat-eaters. Although unintentional, we have managed to squeeze in recipes inspired from Sweden, Morocco, Italy, France, India and Japan. So, regardless of whether it is a birthday party for your sister, your son's school class, or your best friends coming over, we hope that you will find something to put on your dinner table.
– *David*

Sweet Apricot & Cauliflower Dal

HOMEMADE SPICE BLEND
- ½ tbsp coriander seeds
- ½ tsp mustard seeds
- ½ tsp cardamom seeds
- 2 tsp curry powder
- ½ tsp ground cloves
- ½ tsp ground ginger
- a pinch of chili powder
- 6 unsulphured dried apricots, chopped
- 2–3 tbsp ghee (page 25), coconut oil or extra virgin olive oil for frying

- 1 small onion, finely chopped
- 2 garlic cloves, pressed
- 1 cauliflower, cut into florets
- 2 carrots, sliced
- scant 1 cup red lentils, rinsed
- 3 cups coconut milk
- 7 oz spinach, coarsely chopped
- sea salt
- 1 large handful cilantro

Serves 4

I have had a food crush on India for as long as I can remember. I have been there a few times, and am always struck by the huge variety of vegetarian food, based on lentils, beans, potatoes, cauliflower, okra, peas, paneer cheese, fruit and spices. They always manage to combine strong and bold flavors with mild and sweet ones into amazing soups, stews and stir-fries. In this recipe, all the different spices trigger an explosion of flavors, which is rounded off with sweet, dried apricots and coconut milk. We often make our own spice blend, which basically is a way for us to intensify the flavors of the standard supermarket curry powder.
– David

Start by making the spice blend. Grind the first three spices in a mortar with a pestle. Add the rest of the spices and apricots and use your fingers to mix it together.

Heat the ghee in a heavy large saucepan on medium heat. Add the spice blend and stir constantly with a wooden spoon. Fry until it smells fragrant and looks browned, but watch that the spices do not burn. If it looks too dry, add a spoonful, or more, of water.

Add the onion and garlic and fry a couple of minutes while stirring. Add the cauliflower and carrots and stir until they are fully coated by the spices. Now add the lentils, coconut milk, and 1 cup water and stir well. Simmer, covered, for 15–20 minutes or until the vegetables and lentils are cooked through.

Add the spinach and stir to combine. Top with the cilantro and serve the dal on its own or with cooked brown or wild rice. Add salt to taste.

Rhubarb, Apple & Yellow Split Pea Stew

2 tbsp ghee (see page 25), coconut oil or extra virgin olive oil
1 tbsp cumin seeds, ground
1½ tsp cardamom seeds, ground
a pinch of cayenne pepper
1 large onion, diced
4 garlic cloves, crushed
2 in piece of fresh ginger, finely chopped or grated
1 lb 12 oz butternut squash, summer pumpkin or sweet potato, peeled, seeded and cut into 1 in cubes

5 sticks rhubarb (9 oz), sliced
1 red eating apple, cored and diced
⅔ cup yellow split peas or yellow lentils, rinsed
sea salt
2–3 tbsp honey
1 handful of flat-leaf parsley, to garnish, optional

Serves 4–6

Rhubarb is something most people eat for dessert, but its sweet and tangy qualities make it just as good in savory dishes. We learned this from Sarah Britton, our friend, brilliant cook, and My New Roots blogger. This recipe is inspired by hers and I think she was inspired by something Mark Bittman wrote in How to Cook Everything Vegetarian, *so it's really third-hand here.*

We always keep a few boxes of rhubarb in our freezer, so we have been able to make slightly varied versions of this dish all year round. This dish is good on its own, but you can also serve it with cooked brown, black, red or wild rice.

Heat the ghee or oil in a heavy large saucepan over medium heat. Add all the spices and stir constantly with a wooden spoon. Fry until they smell fragrant and look browned – be careful not to let them burn. If it looks too dry, add a spoonful, or more, of water. Add the onion, garlic and ginger and fry for a couple of minutes while stirring.

Add the butternut squash, rhubarb and apple and stir to coat with the spices. Next add the split peas and 4 cups water and simmer, covered, for 20–25 minutes, or until the vegetables and split peas are soft. Season with salt and add the honey.

Serve with a good handful of chopped parsley, if using.

FAMILY DINNERS

Portobello & Peach Burgers

6 portobello mushrooms
6 peaches
6 whole-grain burger buns
3½ oz fresh pea sprouts
5 small tomatoes, sliced
5 small green onions, sliced
1 small handful of thyme leaves

MARINADE
¼ cup extra virgin olive oil
2 sprigs of rosemary (chop leaves from
   1 of them finely; use the other as a
   brush)

1 tbsp chopped fresh thyme leaves
2 garlic cloves, finely chopped
juice of ½ lemon
sea salt and freshly ground black pepper

GUACAMOLE
4 ripe avocados, halved, pitted and
   peeled
3 small tomatoes
1 handful flat-leaf parsley
1 garlic clove, pressed
½ lemon
2 tbsp extra virgin olive oil

Makes 6 burgers

Although over the years we have made several different versions of veggie and bean burgers, patties and cakes, nothing is quite like a grilled portobello mushroom burger. It is the simplest, most natural and delicious piece of food you can put inside a burger bun. It is big, chewy and actually strikingly burger-looking, and when heated it releases moisture and becomes all flavorful and juicy. We like to top our burgers with mashed avocado, fresh tomatoes, sprouts and some kind of fruity salsa. Here we have replaced the salsa with peaches that are grilled with the mushrooms. Serve with our Spicy Skinny Root Sticks (on page 180) and some homemade Apple Ketchup (page 30).

Clean the portobello mushrooms by carefully removing dirt from the caps with a cloth or paper towel; use a little water if necessary. Cut off the stems and discard. Pat dry. Cut the peaches in half and remove the pits.

Make the guacamole – coarsely chop the avocados, tomatoes and parsley. Put them in a small bowl with the pressed garlic, squeeze lemon juice over, add the olive oil and mash everything with a fork. It should be mixed but still a bit chunky. Set aside.

Now make the marinade – pour the olive oil into a small bowl. Add the chopped rosemary, thyme, garlic, freshly squeezed lemon juice and stir to combine. Add salt and pepper to taste. Use the other rosemary sprig to brush the mushrooms and peaches with the marinade.

Preheat a grill pan and grill the mushrooms and peaches for about 3–4 minutes on each side over high heat. Alternatively, you can use an outdoor grill. Use the rosemary sprig to brush the marinade over them as they cook.

Slice the buns in half and toast them lightly on the grill pan or grill. When done, place a big dollop of guacamole on the bottom bun, add pea sprouts, tomatoes, green onion, thyme, one mushroom and two peach halves. Add the top of the bun, and insert a cocktail stick to hold it all together.

Beet Bourguignon

¼ cup extra virgin olive oil, divided
1 yellow onion, chopped
4 garlic cloves, finely chopped
8 small beets, peeled and quartered
  (we used Chioggia beets)
6 carrots, cut into large pieces
3 bay leaves
2 sprigs of thyme
sea salt and freshly ground black
  pepper
2 tbsp tomato paste

1 cup red wine
2¼ cups vegetable stock
2 cups Puy lentils
a pinch of sea salt
2–3 portobello mushrooms, sliced
10 cremini mushrooms
10 pearl onions, peeled
2 tsp arrowroot, dissolved in
  2 tbsp water
a few sprigs of thyme, leaves
  picked, to garnish

Serves 4

Most people are familiar with Julia Child's classic recipe for boeuf bourguignon. Talk about making an impression and leaving a footprint. Her boeuf bourguignon is made with beef and bacon, so not the most appropriate dish for vegetarians, but we reckoned that there must be a way to transform that rich hot pot into something more to our taste. After a few experiments it turns out that we were only one letter away. We turned "beef" into "beet." We also added large chunks of mushrooms to give the stew the right texture and flavor. Our Mashed Roots (on page 149) are also a good companion.

Heat 2 tbsp of the olive oil in a heavy large saucepan or dutch oven over medium heat. Stir in the onion and garlic and sauté until soft. Toss the beets, carrots, bay leaves, thyme and salt and pepper into the pan and cook for 5 minutes, stirring occasionally.

Stir in the tomato paste, red wine and vegetable stock and simmer on low heat for 20 minutes.

Meanwhile, rinse the lentils under running water. Bring 4 cups water and the lentils to a boil. Lower the heat to medium and simmer gently for 15–20 minutes. When almost cooked, add the salt. Drain off any excess water, cover and set aside.

Now heat the remaining 2 tbsp olive oil in a large frying pan, lower the heat and sear the mushrooms and pearl onions, stirring occasionally, until tender and golden in color. Season to taste and set aside.

Taste the stew and add more wine, stock or herbs if you like. Add the arrowroot mixture. Stir gently, just until thickened and clear.

Add the mushrooms and onions and simmer for 10 more minutes. Remove the bay leaves and thyme sprigs before serving. Spoon the stew into 4 bowls together with the lentils, and sprinkle with fresh thyme.

FAMILY DINNERS

Moroccan Vegetable Tagine

3 tbsp extra virgin olive oil
1 large onion, coarsely chopped
3 garlic cloves, pressed
1 in piece fresh ginger, grated
    (or 1 tsp ground)
1–2 tbsp ground cinnamon
1 tsp ground cumin
sea salt
2–3 tsp harissa paste (or dried harissa)
2 x 14 oz cans whole plum tomatoes
grated zest and juice of 1 lemon
1 large handful of cilantro, leaves picked
    and chopped
1 small butternut squash, cut into 2 in
    pieces
1 sweet potato, cut into 2 in pieces

3 carrots, cut into 2 in pieces
1 zucchini, cut into 2 in pieces
10 unsulphured dried apricots
1⅓ cups garbanzo beans, cooked or
    canned and rinsed
½ cup golden raisins

TO SERVE
1 cup whole-grain couscous
2 tbsp olive oil
4 cups boiling water
toasted almonds
1 small handful of fresh cilantro,
    leaves chopped
a few sprigs of fresh mint

Serves 4

Sweet cinnamon is combined with soft vegetables, sweet raisins and hot spices. The trick is to get the vegetables as tender as possible and the easiest way to do that is by letting them slowly steam in their own juices on a low heat for as long as possible. "Tagine" is the name of this type of stew and the domed clay pot that it cooks in. While a traditional tagine is ideal for cooking this recipe, a clay pot or casserole work well. If using a tagine, you might need to soak it before baking. Serve with whole-grain couscous, quinoa or cooked millet.

Heat the olive oil in a heavy large saucepan or flameproof casserole dish and sauté the onion for a few minutes until it softens.

Add the garlic and ginger and the spices and stir before adding the harissa, tomatoes, lemon zest and juice and fresh cilantro. Bring the sauce to a boil and then lower the heat.

Add the squash, sweet potato, carrots, zucchini and apricots. Stir well to coat everything in the tomato sauce. Cover and simmer for about an hour. Keep covered, but stir carefully once or twice while cooking. After an hour and when the vegetables are very tender, stir in the garbanzo beans and raisins and cook for 5 minutes more.

Alternatively, if you are using a tagine: Preheat the oven to 300°F and prepare the tomato sauce as above. Add the vegetables to the tagine, pour over the tomato sauce, making sure all vegetables are covered, attach the lid and put in the oven and cook for about 1½ hours. When the vegetables feel tender, add the garbanzo beans and raisins and let everything cook for 5 minutes more before removing from the oven. When the vegetables are almost ready, place the couscous in a large bowl. Drizzle the olive oil over and stir around until coated. Pour the boiling water over the couscous and cover the bowl with a lid for 10 minutes to allow the couscous to absorb the water. Fluff up the couscous with a fork. Serve immediately with the stew, sprinkled with roasted almonds, coriander and mint.

Hazelnut, Eggplant & Mushroom Parcels

1½ cups hazelnuts, toasted and coarsely chopped
scant ¾ cup raisins
1 eggplant
16 cremini mushrooms

4 sprigs of oregano, leaves picked
scant 1 cup ricotta cheese
juice of ½ lemon
1 tbsp sea salt
freshly ground black pepper

Makes 8, enough for 4 people as a main course

During the summer we often wrap vegetables and fresh herbs in foil and add them to the grill. The intensity of the aroma as we open them always comes as a surprise. Unfortunately the barbecue season is quite short in Sweden, so during the rest of the year we bake these parcels in our oven. We fill them with eggplant, mushrooms, ricotta and hazelnuts, and flavor them with oregano and sweet raisins. They are great at dinner parties as they require little effort. We often serve them with polenta, but a green salad or the potato salad on page 105 would be good for a lighter meal.

Preheat the oven to 400°F. Put the hazelnuts and raisins in a large mixing bowl. Cut the eggplant into ½ in pieces and quarter the mushrooms. Add to the bowl.

Coarsely chop the oregano and add to the bowl, together with the ricotta cheese. Add the lemon juice, salt and pepper. Stir carefully with a wooden spoon until everything is incorporated.

Cut four 10 in squares of parchment paper. Divide the filling between the centers of the parchment paper squares. Gather the corners together and tie the parcels with string. Place on a baking sheet and bake for 25 minutes.

Serve the parcels whole so that your guests can untie their own.

Hash Pan with Fava Beans

1 tbsp extra virgin olive oil
1 yellow onion, coarsely chopped
2 garlic cloves, coarsely chopped
1 lb small summer potatoes, cut into
  ½ in cubes
3 beets, cut into ½ inch cubes
3 carrots, cut into ½ inch cubes
2 parsnips, cut into ½ inch cubes
1 celery root, cut into ½ inch cubes
15 fresh fava beans, shelled and peeled
1 zucchini, cut into 1 in cubes
1 large handful of fresh dill

DRESSING
1 tbsp mustard
2 tbsps extra virgin olive oil
1 tbsp honey or agave syrup
1 tbsp freshly squeezed lemon juice

SERVE WITH
4 organic egg yolks (optional)

Serves 4

*Both Luise and I loved this dish
as children. It's called Biksemad
in Denmark and Pytt i Panna in
Sweden, but is made in exactly the
same way – by chopping up whatever
leftovers you have and frying them
in a pan. Normally it is quite
meat-heavy, with heaps of ham and
sausages. Ours is more root-based.
We use small summer potatoes, beets,
parsnips and celery root. Since some of
the ingredients have different cooking
times, the idea is to chop and throw
in the pan as you go, starting with the
potatoes and ending with the zucchini.
– David*

Heat the olive oil in your largest frying pan on medium heat. Add the
onion and garlic and sauté for about a minute. Add the potatoes and
beets and fry for about 7 minutes before adding the carrots, parsnips
and celery root. Stir occasionally to make sure the roots don't stick to
the pan. Add a little more olive oil if needed. Fry for 5 minutes then add
the fava beans, zucchini and a few sprigs of dill. Fry for 5 more minutes,
or until all the vegetables are tender.

Make the dressing by shaking together the ingredients in a small screw-
topped jar. Add the dressing to the pan if you like it creamy, otherwise
just serve it on the side. Traditionally, this dish is served with an egg yolk
on top. Incorporate it on your plate while the dish still is warm.

Tip: You can use whatever you have in your fridge in this dish. We
sometimes add green onions, garbanzo beans, tofu, broccoli or
sugarsnap peas.

Zucchini Noodles with Marinated Mushrooms

MARINATED MUSHROOMS
4 small portobello mushrooms, sliced
¼ cup extra virgin olive oil
¼ cup apple cider vinegar

CASHEW AND TOMATO DRESSING
1 cup raw cashew nuts, soaked in cold water for 4–6 hours
grated zest and juice of 1 lemon

1 garlic clove, chopped
2 tbsp extra virgin olive oil
generous 1 cup marinated sundried tomatoes, drained
sea salt and freshly ground black pepper

ZUCCHINI NOODLES
2 green or yellow zucchini

Serves 4

You might have heard of zucchini noodles or maybe even tried them? They are thin ribbons of zucchini eaten raw in place of regular spaghetti. This is my favorite way to dress them up. The cashew and sundried tomato dressing is full of flavor and the marinated mushrooms add tanginess and a satisfying chewiness.
– Luise

Place the sliced mushrooms in a bowl. Whisk the oil and vinegar together and pour over the mushrooms. Stir together until the mushrooms are fully coated in the marinade. Cover and leave in the fridge for about an hour, stirring the mushrooms occasionally.

Add all the dressing ingredients to a blender and mix until smooth. If you do not have a blender, grind everything in a large mortar with a pestle until creamy. If it feels too thick, add some water. Season to taste with salt and pepper.

Wash the zucchini and cut them lengthwise, using a julienne or mandolin slicer, so you get thin julienne strips that resemble spaghetti. Put them in a large mixing bowl. Add the dressing and mix gently, so everything is coated. Then add the marinated mushrooms and serve!

Tip: If you don't have a julienne slicer, spiralizer or mandolin slicer, you can use a potato peeler and the "noodles" will come out the size of tagliatelle instead.

Tip: You can slice the zucchini noodles ahead of time and leave them to dry for about 30 minutes before storing in an airtight container in the fridge for up to 5 days.

Sushi Explosion with Wasabi Yogurt

Serves 4

MARINATED TOFU
⅓ cup sesame oil
⅓ cup soy sauce
2 tbsp rice vinegar
1 garlic clove, pressed
½ small red chili, seeded and finely chopped
1 in piece fresh ginger, peeled and grated
10½ oz firm tofu, drained and patted dry with a kitchen towel

BROWN SESAME RICE
2 cups brown, red, or wild rice
a pinch of sea salt
2 tbsp rice vinegar
1 tbsp sesame oil
1 tsp chopped fresh cilantro

PICKLED GINGER
a large chunk of fresh ginger (about 5 in), peeled and thinly sliced lengthwise
¼ cup apple cider vinegar
1 tbsp honey
a pinch of sea salt

WASABI YOGURT
½ cup plain yogurt
1 tbsp green wasabi paste, maybe a little less

SALAD INGREDIENTS
1 large broccoli, cut into florets
1 green onion, thinly sliced
2 avocados, pitted, peeled and cut into cubes
12 cremini mushrooms (or shiitake), quartered
1 handful of sugarsnap peas, halved lengthwise
1 small handful of bean sprouts
½ cucumber, cut into matchsticks
8 sheets nori seaweed, cut into 2x2-inch squares
1 tiny handful toasted sesame seeds
1 large handful cilantro leaves

This is what happened one day when we felt like making our own vegetarian sushi, but were too lazy to go through the whole Japanese rice and roll procedure. Instead we marinated tofu, boiled some brown rice, chopped our favorite vegetables, cut the seaweed into pieces and made it look like the sushi had "exploded" into a bowl. We love this salad. The sesame oil, rice vinegar and seaweed give the salad that sushi feeling, but with a more nourishing twist.

MARINATING THE TOFU
Cut the tofu into 1 in cubes. Combine the remaining marinade ingredients in a bowl and add the tofu. Mix until well coated. Chill for at least 25 minutes (longer if you have the time).

PREPARING THE RICE
Rinse the rice in water until the water runs clear, drain and add to a saucepan with 4¼ cups water and the salt. Bring to a boil. Reduce the heat and simmer for 45 minutes or until tender and the water has been absorbed. Cool slightly and stir in the rice vinegar, sesame oil and cilantro.

PREPARING THE PICKLED GINGER
Place the ginger slices on a plate, sprinkle with sea salt and set aside for 15–30 minutes. Squeeze the ginger with your hands, rinse it under running water and squeeze again. Place in a small bowl.

Whisk the remaining ingredients together with 2 tbsp water and pour over the ginger slices. Pickle for 15–30 minutes.

PREPARING THE WASABI YOGURT

Stir the yogurt and half of the wasabi paste together. Taste and add more wasabi if you like – the flavor of the wasabi can vary quite a bit depending on the brand you use.

ASSEMBLY

Blanch the broccoli: Place the florets in a bowl and pour boiled water over, let sit for 2 minutes, then drain and rinse in ice-cold water.
Combine all the vegetables and nori together in a bowl.
Divide the rice into 4 large bowls and top with the vegetables and the marinated tofu. Drizzle some of the tofu marinade over each salad and top with sesame seeds and cilantro. Serve with the marinated ginger, wasabi yogurt and some soy sauce.

Sicilian Parmigiana Di Zucchine

1 batch Basic Tomato Sauce, with
   a handful of mint added with
   the basil (see page 22),
5 zucchini
5 eggs, hard-boiled
2 tbsp extra virgin olive oil

10½ oz buffalo mozzarella, drained
   and sliced
3½ oz/1 cup grated Parmesan cheese
1 large handful of basil, leaves picked
1 large handful of mint, leaves picked
sea salt and freshly ground black pepper

Serves 4–6

*This is a classic Italian recipe,
simililar to lasagna but layered with
zucchini slices instead of sheets of
pasta. It is therefore a bit lighter and
yet very nourishing. We use a Sicilian-
inspired tomato sauce with lots of fresh
mint added to it. It's a wonderful and
unexpected flavor combination.*
*We took a shot of the dish (opposite)
before adding the top layer of tomato
sauce and Parmesan cheese, so you can
see how the layers should look.*

Preheat the oven to 400°F. Thinly slice the zucchini lengthwise, about
⅓ in thick. Place in a large colander, sprinkle with 5 tsp of salt and toss
well. Set aside to drain for 30 minutes.

Meanwhile, crack and peel the eggs and cut into ⅓ in slices. Rinse the
zucchini slices and pat dry with paper towels. Preheat the grill. Brush
the slices with the olive oil and grill for 10 minutes or until golden,
turning once. You can also use a grill pan to do this.

To assemble the dish, ladle a little tomato sauce into a 10 x 12 in baking
dish. Cover with a layer of zucchini, then mozzarella slices, egg slices,
Parmesan, basil leaves, mint leaves and pepper. Then repeat. You want
to finish with a layer of courgette and then cover completely with the
last of the tomato sauce and the Parmesan.

Bake in the oven for 40 minutes or until the cheese is golden and
bubbling. Remove from the oven and let it set for about 15 minutes
before serving.

Red Lentil Polpette with Lemon Balm Sauce

1 cup red lentils
½ red onion, finely chopped
2 garlic cloves, minced
3 tbsp extra virgin olive oil
2 tbsp tomato paste
⅓ cup rolled oats
1 tsp paprika
a pinch of cayenne pepper, or more
   to taste
sea salt

LEMON BALM AND BASIL SAUCE
1 handful of lemon balm, leaves
   picked
1 handful of basil, leaves picked
¼ cup oil of choice
juice of ½ lemon
1 small handful of hazelnuts, toasted
   and skinned
sea salt and freshly ground black
   pepper

Makes 15

One day I came home from work and Luise had prepared these vegan polpette, served with zucchini noodles. It was her own version of the spaghetti and meatballs from Lady and the Tramp. *I adore her for things like that. Although I have been a vegetarian for more than half my life, I have never done anything even slightly similar. And she just threw it together on a regular Tuesday night. Such an innovative take on an old classic. The lentils add a nice, sweet flavor and texture to the polpette, and go really well with the lemon balm and basil sauce. Serve with Zucchini Noodles (page 131), or with regular whole-grain spaghetti.*
– David

To prepare the polpette, rinse the lentils and place in a saucepan with 2¼ cups cold water. Bring to a boil, then reduce the heat and simmer gently for 15 minutes or until tender. Drain well and cool slightly.

Mash the lentils with a fork or use an immersion/hand blender. The consistency you want is mashed but still with some lentils left whole. Place in a mixing bowl, add the remaining polpette ingredients and stir with a spoon until everything is combined. Place in the fridge for 30 minutes.

Preheat the oven to 375°F and line a baking sheet with parchment paper. Form 15 balls with your hands, place them on the baking sheet and bake for 15–20 minutes. Turn every 5 minutes to get a nice even color and shape.

Meanwhile, make the lemon balm and basil sauce. Place all the ingredients in a blender with 2 tablespoons of water and mix until creamy. If you prefer the sauce a little thinner, add some water.

Tip: If you can't find lemon balm, use more basil and add the juice of one lemon.

Tip: For a gluten-free alternative, use gluten-free oats.

FAMILY DINNERS

Four Vegetarian Pizzas

BASIC SPELT PIZZA DOUGH
1 cup lukewarm water
2 tsp active dry yeast
2 tsp sea salt
2½ cups light spelt flour
2 tbsp olive oil

Makes 12 mini pizzas or 2 large

You know when you do something that you think you are pretty good at and then you see someone else doing it a hundred times better? That is how we felt when we ordered a vegetarian pizza from a small ristorante on Sicily, a few years back. Mama mia, *it was a taste sensation! And they had thrown at least 15 different vegetables on a small pizza slice. Ever since our visit, we have been working on improving our own pizza recipes. Here we have made a few favorite combinations into mini pizzas. The amounts for the toppings are enough to make 2 large or 12 small pizzas, so just adjust them if you want to make more than one kind. If you want a lighter, gluten-free pizza crust, try our cauliflower "dough" on page 86.*

Pour the lukewarm water in a medium bowl. Add the yeast and salt and stir to combine. Mix in 2 cups of the flour. Gradually stir in the rest of the flour until the dough forms a ball. Knead on a floured work surface for a couple of minutes, adding more flour if it sticks to your hands. Put the dough back in the bowl and rub with the olive oil. Rub the dough until it's completely covered in the oil. Cover the bowl with plastic wrap and leave in a warm place for 1–2 hours.

Preheat the oven to 475°F. Knead the dough with your hands on a lightly floured work surface. Divide it into 10 to 12 small portions. Stretch and flatten the dough until you get the desired size and thickness that you prefer and place on baking sheets lined with parchment paper. Spelt flour doesn't stretch as easily as wheat flour but if you work carefully and flatten it with the palm of your hand you will get it right. Another trick is to roll them out directly on the parchment paper with a lightly floured rolling pin and then just transfer the parchment paper to the baking sheet.

Add the topping of your choice and bake for about 10–15 minutes until golden around the edges.

Red Sicilian Topping

½ batch Basic Tomato Sauce (page 22)
6 small potatoes, halved and boiled
12 slices marinated and grilled eggplant (buy ready-made or use recipe on page 149)
12 cherry tomatoes, halved
12 mushrooms, halved
1 handful of pickled capers, drained
6 small green onions, halved lengthwise
2 sprigs of oregano, leaves picked

Smear about 2 tablespoons tomato sauce on each pizza dough round. Divide the potatoes, eggplant, cherry tomatoes, mushrooms and capers among the pizzas. Add the green onions and oregano leaves and bake for about 10–15 minutes until golden around the edges. You can also just use the tomato sauce, cherry tomatoes and oregano to make a simple and pretty cherry tomato pizza.

Sweet Apricot Topping

1 cup ricotta cheese
12 fresh apricots, pitted and sliced
1½ cups fresh raspberries
½ cup Raw Date Syrup (page 30)

Smear a heaping tablespoon of ricotta on each pizza dough round. Brush the apricot slices with date sauce and arrange them in a circular pattern on each pizza. Sprinkle some raspberries over each one, then bake for about 10–15 minutes until golden around the edges.

Green Zucchini Topping

7 oz/4 cups baby spinach
½ cup olive oil
2 garlic cloves
salt and freshly ground black pepper
12 small zucchini, sliced

3½ oz/scant ½ cup soft goat cheese, crumbled

This pizza has a green sauce that can be prepared in a flash, no cooking needed. Combine the spinach, olive oil, ¼ cup water, garlic, salt and pepper in a blender, and purée until smooth. Smear the spinach sauce evenly over the pizza dough rounds. Arrange the zucchini slices on top of the sauce, sprinkle with crumbled goat cheese and bake for about 10–15 minutes until golden around the edges.

White Potato Topping

1 tbsp extra virgin olive oil
12 potatoes, unpeeled, sliced
2 small green onions, thinly sliced
6 sprigs oregano or rosemary, leaves picked

3½ oz/scant ½ cup soft goat cheese, crumbled
salt and freshly ground black pepper

Brush each pizza dough round with a thin layer of olive oil. Cover each with potato slices, green onion, oregano, goat cheese, salt and freshly ground black pepper. Drizzle a bit of olive oil over the pizzas and bake for about 10-15 minutes until the outer part of the topping and the edges are slightly burnt.

Mascarpone "Beanotto" with Oyster Mushrooms & Spinach

2 tbsp extra virgin olive oil
1 large onion, finely chopped
2 garlic cloves, finely chopped
3½ oz/1½ cups sliced oyster or button
  mushrooms
½ cup dry white wine
9 oz spinach, coarsely chopped

2⅔ cups cooked white cannellini beans
  (see page 28)
½ cup vegetable stock
¼ cup mascarpone cheese
grated zest and juice of ½ lemon
1 handful of thyme, leaves picked
sea salt and freshly ground black pepper

Serves 4

Risotto has always been a hit in our family, especially during the autumn and winter months. But sometimes we prefer to cook completely grain-free dishes, and then these creamy beans hit the spot. We call this dish "beanotto" because the wine flavors and the creamy consistency are very similar to a risotto. If you use pre-boiled or canned beans, this dish will be ready in 10 minutes.

Heat the olive oil in a large saucepan over medium heat. Add the onion and garlic. Sauté for a few minutes, stirring occasionally, until softened and golden.

Add the mushrooms and fry for about a minute. Stir in the wine and spinach and simmer until the spinach has cooked down.

Now add the beans and stock. Cook, stirring, for 3–4 minutes. Reduce the heat and add the mascarpone cheese, lemon juice and thyme. Stir well, then taste and season with salt and pepper. Serve sprinkled with grated lemon zest.

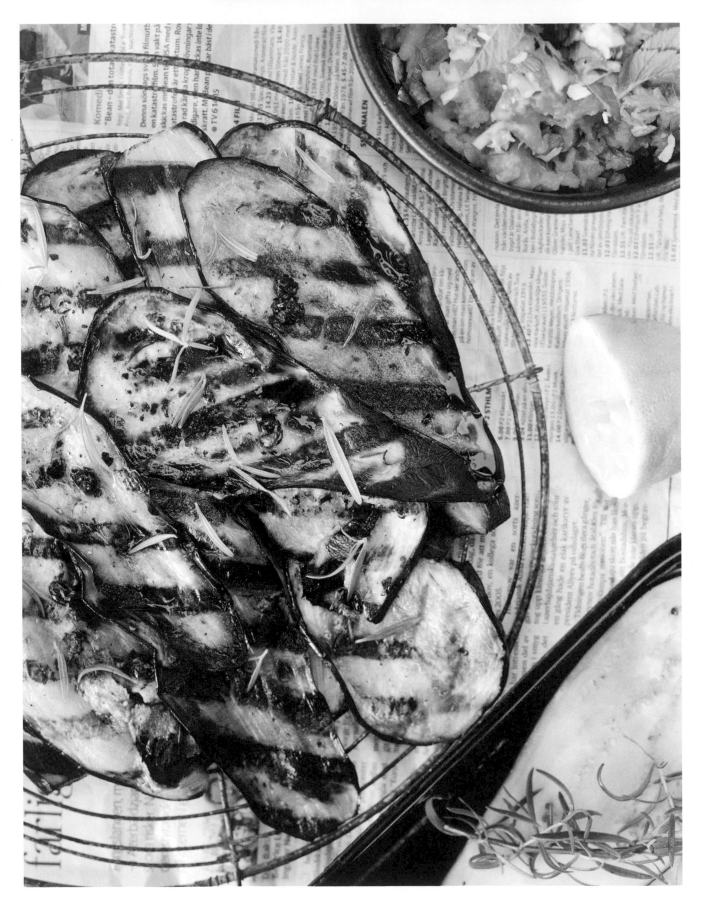

Juniper-marinated Eggplant & Mashed Roots

MASHED ROOTS
2 lbs 3 oz mix of sweet potato, parsnip and turnip
⅓ cup olive oil
grated zest and juice of 1 lemon
a handful of cilantro or flat-leaf parsley
scant ½ cup coarsely chopped almonds or pecans
sea salt and freshly ground black pepper

JUNIPER MARINADE
1 tbsp dried juniper berries, crushed
2–3 sprigs rosemary, leaves picked
½ cup extra virgin olive oil
juice of 1 lemon
sea salt and freshly ground black pepper
3–4 small eggplants, cut lengthwise into slices about ½ in thick

Serves 4

The root season in Sweden is endless. They are one of the few kinds of vegetables that can actually handle this climate. We often pound them into a lemon- and almond-flavored root mash. You can make it using a food processor, but it's even better mashed by hand, with a little bit of texture left. During the summer we serve it with juniper-marinated eggplant slices, chargrilled just a tad too long for depth of flavor.

Rinse and peel the root vegetables, and cut into small pieces. Place in a large saucepan, cover with cold water and bring to a boil. Lower the heat and gently simmer for about 15–20 minutes or until tender; cooking time will depend on the size of your vegetables. If a knife goes through easily, they are cooked.

Remove from the heat, reserve a little of the cooking water and drain off the rest. Add the oil, lemon zest and juice, cilantro, nuts and salt and pepper to the pan and use a potato masher to mash the roots well. Use a wooden spoon to beat further, adding a splash of cooking water to achieve the consistency you desire.

Meanwhile, mix the crushed juniper berries and rosemary leaves with the oil and lemon juice to make the marinade. Season with salt and pepper. Lay the eggplant slices on a large plate or tray and cover with the marinade. Leave for 30 minutes to 1 hour to really soak up the flavors.

Preheat your grill or grill pan until it is almost smoking. Grill the marinated eggplant on each side, turning every minute or so. Use a rosemary sprig to brush them with more marinade. They are ready when they are soft in the middle with crispy sides and charred in stripes. Serve with the root mash and a green salad.

You will also need:
5 pieces of cheesecloth or muslin (8 x 12 in)
10 2-in lengths of kitchen string

Quinoa & Vegetable Chorizo Salad

Serves 4

A word of warning: This recipe uses words that might freak out some vegetarians. But fear not – our chorizos are purely plant-based! This is without a doubt the most unexpected dish in this cookbook. Not only have we made sausages(!) but we also threw them in a quinoa salad. It's definitely not our usual combination, but it is really good. The mustard dressing in the salad perfectly complements the chorizos. You can, of course, also make the quinoa salad without the chorizos (or buy ready-made). And equally, there are many ways you can eat and serve the vegetable chorizos – as a classic hot dog, in bangers and mash, or in a stew.

VEGETABLE CHORIZOS
- scant ½ cup sundried tomatoes, rinsed
- ¾ cup cashew nuts, toasted
- ½ red onion, coarsely chopped
- ½ small red chili, seeded and finely chopped
- 6 unsulphured dried apricots, coarsely chopped
- 2 sprigs of oregano, leaves picked and chopped
- 1 cup rice flour
- 1 tbsp xanthan gum
- 1 tbsp flax seeds, ground
- ¼ cup extra virgin olive oil
- 4¼ cups vegetable stock
- 1 tbsp olive oil, for frying

QUINOA SALAD
- 1 cup black quinoa
- 15 cherry tomatoes, halved
- 2 small red apples, diced
- ½ onion, sliced
- 2 cups cooked lima beans (see page 28)

DRESSING
- ⅓ cup olive oil
- zest and juice of ½ lemon
- 3 tbsp hot English mustard
- sea salt
- a few sprigs of oregano, to garnish

To prepare the chorizos, combine the sundried tomatoes, cashew nuts, onion, chili and apricots in a food processor or blender. Pulse until finely chopped. Add the chopped oregano, rice flour, xanthan gum and flax seed and pulse until everything is combined. Add the olive oil and ¼ cup water and pulse until a dough is formed. It should be easy to handle and form into a sausage shape.

Divide the dough into 5 equal parts. Roll each piece into a sausage, place on a piece of cheesecloth, roll up and tie both ends firmly with a piece of twine.

Bring the vegetable stock to a boil in a large, wide saucepan or sauté pan. Lay the chorizos in it and let them boil for about 45 minutes. Next, carefully remove the cheesecloth from the boiled chorizos. Heat the olive oil in a frying pan on medium-high heat and fry the chorizos until they are nicely browned all over.

Next, prepare the quinoa salad. Place 2¼ cups water, the quinoa and a pinch of salt in a heavy saucepan. Bring to a boil, lower the heat and gently simmer for 15–20 minutes. Drain any excess water and set aside to cool. Slice the fried chorizos.

Whisk together the dressing ingredients in a small bowl. Put the quinoa, tomatoes, apples, onions and lima beans in a large bowl. Add the chorizo slices then pour over the dressing and toss until all the ingredients are well coated. Garnish with oregano and serve.

Amaranth & Halloumi-stuffed Tomatoes

STUFFED TOMATOES

1 cup amaranth
a pinch of sea salt
½ cup coarsley chopped raw shelled
  pistachio nuts
3½ oz halloumi cheese,
  coarsely chopped
3 tbsp pickled capers, drained
1 large egg
6–8 large tomatoes

ROASTED ROOTS

2 lb 3 oz mixed root vegetables,
  such as sweet potato, parsnip
  and carrots
generous 1 cup black olives
3 sprigs of rosemary
2 tbsp extra virgin olive oil
2 tsp sea salt
1 lemon, quartered
1 garlic bulb, halved horizontally

Serves 4

We love efficient cooking. In this recipe the root vegetables are roasted in the same pan with the stuffed tomatoes. Everything is ready at the same time, which always makes things easier, and the filling can be prepared a day in advance and stored in the fridge. Amaranth is a tiny, protein-packed seed that makes this dish lighter than the traditionally used rice. If you can't find amaranth use quinoa or millet instead. If you can't find halloumi cheese, use a feta cheese instead.

Place the amaranth in a saucepan with 2½ cups water and the salt. Bring to a boil, lower the heat to a bare simmer, cover and cook gently for 20 minutes.

Meanwhile, combine the chopped pistachio nuts, halloumi cheese, capers, and egg in a medium-sized mixing bowl. Drain the cooked amaranth and cool slightly before adding to the bowl with other ingredients. Stir to combine and set aside.

Use a sharp knife to cut off a cap from the top of each tomato. Carefully lift it off and remove the seeds and pulp from inside using a teaspoon. Fill the tomato shells with the amaranth mixture, dividing evenly, and pop the caps back on.

Preheat the oven to 400°F.

Rinse the roots. (If using organic, there is no need to peel them.) Cut all the vegetables into 2 x ½ in pieces. Place them in a large mixing bowl, together with the olives, rosemary, oil and salt. Toss, using your hands, to coat with oil. Place on a baking sheet, together with the stuffed tomatoes, garlic and lemon quarters, and put in the oven. Roast for 50–60 minutes, or until golden with crispy edges. Serve immediately.

Small Bites

Every once in a while, we do an "Extreme Fridge Makeover." We empty it, clean it and David rearranges the shelves so that we, "for the first time," will have complete order in there. The air is filled with excitement as he explains the new strategy: "Okay Lul, listen now, vegetables go here, leftovers on the top shelf. And all your jars have their own shelf right here." He is good at planning stuff like that. And I can really see it working, in theory. The problem is that we are no good at following those instructions and in the midst of cleaning up after dinner, if I see an empty shelf, I go for it. And so does David, no matter what he claims. So six months later, we have to start all over again.

My jars are definitely also part of the problem – the spreads, compotes, pâtés, nut butters, fermented cabbage and homemade sweeteners tend to multiply all over the shelves. I imagine that a good solution would be to get an extra fridge, just for all our jars. The thing is, we don't eat like traditional families. Many of our meals are accompanied by a side or a spread of some sort. Raw vegetable sticks, a bowl of goat cheese dip, some beans on the side or a jar of baba ganoush. It's often all those bits and pieces that add up to a whole and satisfying meal.

We have collected a few of our favorite "jars" here, but also a recipe for grain-free seed crackers, an unexpected ceviche and a plate of zucchini and ricotta rolls. All of these small bites are not only good as side dishes, but would also be perfect on a buffet table.
– *Luise*

Baba Ganoush

2 eggplants (approx 1 lb 12 oz)
2 tbsp sesame oil
2 tbsp olive oil
3 tbsp freshly squeezed lemon juice
2 garlic cloves, pressed
1 tsp sea salt
1 bunch of flat-leaf parsley or cilantro,
   leaves picked

Makes enough to fill 1 x 12 oz jar

Middle Eastern cuisine has so many great vegetarian spreads. Hummus is, of course, the most popular and well-known. But we'd like to highlight another favorite of ours: baba ganoush. Its slightly tangy and smoky flavors go particularly well with pita chips and other salt crackers. Most recipes call for tahini, but since it has a tendency to overpower all the other flavors, we use the milder sesame oil instead.

Preheat the oven to 475°F.

Halve each eggplant lengthwise. Place them cut-sides down on a baking sheet lined with parchment paper and roast for about 45 minutes, until completely soft with black skin. They will look punctured when they're done.

Remove from the oven and leave to cool for a few minutes. Remove the skin and discard. It should come away easily, but if not, seal the eggplant in a plastic bag for 10 min to steam and then try again.

Finely chop the pulp and scrape into a medium-sized bowl. Add the sesame and olive oils, lemon juice, garlic, salt, and parsley. Stir and mash everything with a fork until smooth. Taste and add more salt and lemon juice if necessary.

Chill for about 1 hour before serving. Store in an airtight glass jar in the fridge. Keeps for 3–4 days.

Smashed Peas with Almonds & Chili

3½ cups shelled fresh peas, or frozen (thawed)
½ cup coarsely chopped almonds
juice of ½ lemon
1–2 tsp seeded and finely chopped fresh red chili
1 small bunch of mint, leaves picked (reserve a few for serving)
¼ cup extra virgin olive oil
sea salt

Serves 4

For some reason, we don't use peas very often. It's strange considering their sweet flavor and pretty color. We were reminded of this when we visited a garden cafe on the island of Gotland in southern Sweden. They had a pea mash that tasted so good smeared on a slice of sourdough. As soon as we returned home, we went to the market, bought a big bag of fresh peas and made this dish. Use it as a side dish or smear it on sourdough or rye bread (page 58).

Place all the ingredients in a mixing bowl. Use a hand/immersion blender to purée the peas, but keep some whole to create a rough-textured mash. Taste and adjust the seasoning. Top with a few mint leaves and serve. The color of the peas darkens rather quickly, so this is best eaten on the day it's made.

Fig, Rhubarb & Pear Compote

5 oz rhubarb (about 3 sticks), cut into
  1 in pieces
2 pears, peeled, cored and coarsely
  chopped
6 soft dried figs, coarsely chopped
1 in piece of fresh ginger, grated
1 tbsp cardamom seeds, ground

Makes about 1¼ cups

*Even though we don't use sugar
in this compote, it is very sweet and
super delicious. The flavors are far
more complex than a traditional
strawberry compote, and it therefore
goes really well with a cheese and seed
crackers or crisp bread.*

Place the fruit, ginger, cardamom and 1 tablespoon water in a medium-sized saucepan. Slowly bring to a boil (the heat will release the juices from the fruit), lower the heat and gently simmer for 30 minutes, stirring occasionally until thick and pulpy.
Remove from the heat and leave to cool. Store in an airtight glass jar in the fridge. Keeps for about a week.

163   SMALL BITES

Orange-kissed Seed Crackers

½ cup sunflower seeds
½ cup sesame seeds
⅓ cup flax seeds, ground
½ cup hemp seeds
scant 1 cup amaranth flour
   (or quinoa flour or almond flour)
1½ tsp sea salt
¼ cup olive oil
2 tbsp freshly squeezed orange juice
1 tbsp honey or maple syrup

Makes about 20

These gluten-free and nut-free multi-seed crackers are almost too easy to make – no kneading or leavening needed. Just stir the ingredients together, flatten out on a pan and bake. You will end up with delicious crispy crackers that are great with any of the spreads in this chapter. If you can't find hemp seeds increase the amount of sunflower seeds. If you like your seeds natural omit the orange juice and honey.

Preheat the oven to 300°F.

Combine all the seeds in a medium bowl. Scoop out about a quarter of the seeds and reserve for the topping. Add flour, salt and olive oil to the bowl with 1¼ cups water. Using a wooden spoon, stir to combine. You should have a loose batter. If it is not loose enough, add some more water; it will evaporate as you bake the crackers.

Line 2 12 x 14 in baking sheets with parchment paper. Pour the batter over the paper on each pan, dividing evenly. Use a spatula to spread the batter as thinly as you can.

Bake in the oven for 25 minutes.

Meanwhile, whisk together the honey and orange juice in a small bowl. Remove the baking sheet from the oven, brush the cracker with the orange glaze and sprinkle with the reserved seeds. Cut into 2 in pieces and bake for 30 minutes more or until they are crunchy. Cool on a wire rack.

Sprout Ceviche

grated zest and juice of 3 limes
1 shallot, finely chopped
2 tbsp extra virgin olive oil
½ tsp sea salt
½ tsp seeded and finely chopped
   fresh red chili
1 large handful of cilantro leaves
2¼ cups sprouted mung beans
   (page 28), or use store-bought

Serves 4

Even though we don't eat fish at home, we love marinating all kinds of vegetables in fresh ceviche flavors. It can be anything from a more complex ceviche salad to a simple side dish, like this one. Sprouts work particularly well with the ceviche treatment, as they really soak up the flavors. If making this for a buffet, it would look pretty to serve a spoonful of sprouts in endive leaves. Or just scoop a spoonful onto your plate as a side dish.

Put the lime zest and juice, onion, olive oil, salt and chili in a mixing bowl and stir to combine. Add the sprouts and cilantro and give it another stir. Leave for 15 minutes before serving to intensify the flavors.

Tip: Try using fresh green peas, shredded cucumber, fresh corn or alfalfa sprouts instead of mung bean sprouts.

Zucchini Rolls with Passion Fruit & Lemon Ricotta

2 zucchini
2 tsp sea salt
extra virgin olive oil, for brushing
1 cup ricotta cheese
5 passion fruit (or about ½ cup
 thawed pulp if using frozen)
juice of ½ lemon
1 handful of basil leaves,
 coarsely chopped
freshly ground black pepper

Makes about 12 rolls

If you have been reading and trying a few of our recipes, you might have noticed our slight obsession with lemon. Whenever we feel that something is missing in a recipe, we tend to reach for a lemon. Lemon pairs particularly well with ricotta, but, then again, we think it tastes great with almost anything. These rolls looks pretty impressive on a buffet table, but are surprisingly simple to make. If you can't find passion fruits, use frozen pulp or finely chopped mango.

Thinly slice the zucchini lengthwise, about ¼ in thick. Place the slices in a large colander, sprinkle with the salt and toss well. Set aside to drain for 30 minutes. Rinse well.

Transfer the zucchini slices to a clean tea towel, pat dry and brush the cut sides with olive oil. Heat a grill pan on medium-high heat and grill the slices for 4 minutes on each side, or until tender and grill marks appear. Set aside to cool.

Put the ricotta in a mixing bowl. Cut the passion fruits in half and scoop out the seeds and pulp of 3 of them into the mixing bowl. Add the lemon juice, basil, salt and pepper and mix everything together.

Put 1 tablespoon of the ricotta mixture at the end of each zucchini slice. Roll up and place on a serving plate. Repeat with the remaining slices. Top with seeds and pulp from the remaining 2 passion fruits.

Red Pepper & Rosemary Spread

3 large red bell peppers, halved and
  seeded
⅔ cup sunflower seeds
a pinch of cayenne pepper
sea salt
juice of ½ lemon
2 sprigs of rosemary, leaves picked

Makes about 1 cup

When roasted, the peppers lose all their bite and acidity and take on a very round, almost smoky flavor, which pairs well with toasted sunflower seeds and a hint of cayenne. Although good on a sandwich, this spread has far more uses than that. It magically pairs with almost anything savory that we make, so it is one of the jars in our fridge that always goes from full to empty in no time.

Preheat the oven to 400°F.

Place the peppers on a baking sheet and roast for about 40 minutes, or until slightly charred. Remove from the oven and leave to cool. Meanwhile, briefly toast the sunflower seeds, cayenne and salt in a dry frying pan over medium heat. When the peppers have cooled, peel the skin away. Chop the peppers and place in a food processor or blender; add the toasted sunflower seed mixture, lemon juice and rosemary, and purée until smooth. Taste and adjust the seasoning if necessary. Transfer to an airtight glass jar. Keeps in the fridge for up to 2 weeks.

Sage & Walnut Pâté

1 cup sundried tomatoes in oil (15–20),
    drained (if not in oil, soak them in
    water until soft)
7 oz/2 cups walnuts, soaked in cold
    water for 6–8 hours or overnight
10 sage leaves, chopped
sea salt and freshly ground black pepper

Makes about 2 cups

It's not often that we envy meat-eaters, but when it comes to things to put on bread, vegetarian options are much more limited (unless you like fake ham). Sure, we have cheese, fruit compote and peanut butter. But we sometimes crave something more savory, so then we make this pâté. It's great on a piece of rye (page 58) or crispbread (page 48).

Combine all the ingredients with 2 tbsp water in a food processor or use an immersion / hand blender. Blend until smooth. Add a little more water if necessary to form a thick paste. Transfer to airtight glass jars. Keeps in the fridge for about a week.

Broccoli Pesto

1 large head of broccoli, florets and stems chopped
3 sprigs of basil or sage, leaves picked
juice of ½ lemon

¾ cup hazelnuts, toasted (or toasted chickpeas)
2 garlic cloves, peeled
½ cup extra virgin olive oil
sea salt
freshly ground black pepper

Makes about 2 cups

Broccoli is one of those vegetables that most people want to cook, but we actually prefer it raw. This recipe and the broccoli salad on page 68 are two examples of how good it can be uncooked. We have omitted the cheese usually found in pestos, but if you are not vegan, a few slices of Pecorino Romano work great here.

Combine all the ingredients in a blender or food processor with 2 tbsp water and purée until smooth, stopping and scraping down the sides as necessary. Taste and adjust the seasoning. Add more olive oil or water if it feels too dry and more nuts or chickpeas if it is too runny. Transfer to airtight glass jars. Keeps in the fridge for a few days. Serve as a spread or with pasta.

Crunchy Curried Egg Salad

6 eggs (at room temperature)
1 small handful of pumpkin seeds, toasted
1 red apple, halved, cored and cut into ½ in cubes
10 radishes, thinly sliced
5 asparagus spears, cut into ½ in pieces
1 large bunch of chives, snipped (reserve a few for serving, including chive flowers when in season)

FOR THE DRESSING
½ cup plain yogurt
2 tbsp mayonnaise (optional)
1 tsp curry powder (or more to taste)
a pinch of cayenne pepper
sea salt

Serves 4

Egg salad is an essential topping on the Danish open rye sandwiches called Smørrebrød. It's traditionally quite heavy, so we usually make a lighter version using yogurt, crunchy fruit and vegetables. Serve on top of the Dark Danish Rye Bread on page 58.

Place the eggs (using a spoon!) into a pan of boiling water. Reduce the heat to medium and gently boil for 7–8 minutes. Remove the eggs from the heat and place the pan under cold running water.

Toast the pumpkin seeds in a frying pan.

Prepare the curry dressing by whisking all ingredients together in a small bowl and set aside.

When the eggs have cooled, crack and peel each egg and chop into ½ in cubes. Put into a bowl with all of the remaining egg salad ingredients. Stir gently with a large spoon (you don't want to mash the eggs) so all ingredients are well coated in curry dressing. Put a nice handful of chives on top and serve.

SMALL BITES

Spicy Skinny Root Sticks

500 g (1 lb 2oz) root vegetables,
    such as carrots, sweet potatoes,
    parsnips, turnips
2 tbsp extra virgin olive oil
a pinch chili powder, or more to taste
1 tsp sea salt

Serves 4

We don't eat a lot of French fries at home, but that will hardly come as a surprise. However, when we do, we often make these instead of the traditional deep-fried version. They are perfectly crisp and crunchy, even though they are only baked – all thanks to how thinly they are sliced. These are great with our Portobello and Peach Burgers on page 118.

Preheat the oven to 400°F.

Wash and peel the root vegetables, or leave the skins on for a crunchier texture. Slice them into ⅛ in-thick slices, lengthwise, then stack the slices and cut them into ⅛ in-thick sticks. Pat dry using paper towels and place in a large mixing bowl.

Add the olive oil, chili powder and salt and toss so every single stick is coated. Place the root sticks on two baking sheets lined with parchment paper. Make sure you spread them out in a single layer. Bake for about 8 minutes, or until golden with crisp, brown ends. Since we use different roots, the baking time can vary slightly. Keep an eye on the oven, and remove any that are already done.

Drinks

"My favorite drink? Ha, that's easy! The juice of a sweet Sicilian blood orange, squeezed into a glass. I can't think of anything better. No, wait. Two Swedish apples, from your aunt's tree, pushed through the juicer with a knob of ginger. That is my favorite drink. No, no, now I know, the simple cane juice from that street vendor in Saigon, or maybe th—" "Well, there you have it," David interrupts me.

Well, exactly. I asked him how I should start this chapter. And he has got a point; I have a drinking problem. I love all the possibilities that come from mixing fresh fruit and vegetables into juices, smoothies, shakes and lassis. Why should I choose just one? And no wonder we have worn out three blenders and one juicer in three years.

We make juices for breakfast, juices for sweetening food and desserts, and juices to use in smoothies. You can even turn an unexpected vegetable like broccoli into the most delicious drink, just by balancing its flavors with a little sweet and some tanginess. Apple, lemon and ginger usually do the trick. In this chapter, we have rounded up a few of our best juice and smoothie recipes. And we have included an alcohol-free cocktail, an elderflower lemonade and two Indian drinks, one warm and one cold. See if you can choose just one favorite!
– *Luise*

Bubbling Kombucha Cocktail

FOR THE KOMBUCHA
⅓ cup sugar (we use brown)
2 green or black teabags
1 Kombucha "mushroom" +
  ½ cup liquid culture (it will
  come with the mushroom)

FOR THE COCKTAIL
1 cup Kombucha brew
1 cup unsweetened apple juice
½ cup crushed ice
2 thinly sliced rhubarb sticks

Serves 2

Kombucha is a fermented, enzyme- and probiotic-rich tea, which you either can make yourself or buy pre-made in health stores. You can drink it as it is, add it to smoothies or even make it into ice pops. We love the bubbles you find naturally in kombucha. They add a festive touch to a fruity, alcohol-free summer cocktail. If you do not start a new batch right away, you need to rinse out the mushroom jars every 4 weeks. Just put the mushroom and culture into a bowl while rinsing the jars with hot water, and then pour them back into their jars. Store at room temperature.

TO MAKE THE KOMBUCHA

Boil 4¼ cups water and let it cool slightly. Pour into a large glass jar, add the sugar and stir until it has dissolved. Add the tea and steep for 15 minutes.

Remove the teabags and let the mixture cool to 75°F. It is important to measure the temperature – if it is too hot you will kill the mushroom. Place the Kombucha mushroom and culture in the cooled tea mixture, cover with muslin or cheesecloth, secure with a rubber band and keep in a warm room (temperature around 75–80°F) for 8–14 days. By this time it will probably have produced a baby mushroom on the surface, small bubbles will start to show and the liquid will taste vinegary. If it is still very sweet, leave it for another week or so.

When ready, remove the baby mushroom and the mother mushroom using a wooden or plastic spoon (do not use metal), and rinse them under lukewarm water. Place each mushroom in a separate glass jar together with half a cup of the kombucha culture (the one you just made) and cover. Pour the remaining newly brewed kombucha into bottles and store in the fridge for up to 1 month.

TO MAKE THE COCKTAIL

Mix the 1 cup kombucha brew and apple juice in a large jug with the ice. Crush half the rhubarb slices with the back of a knife. Stir all of the rhubarb slices into the jug and serve immediately.

Chocolate & Blackberry Milkshake

16 fresh blackberries
  (or thawed if frozen)
2 frozen bananas (or fresh bananas
  and 2 ice cubes)
1 cup coconut milk
½ cup oat milk (page 27)
  or milk of your choice
3 tbsp cacoa powder
1 tbsp cacao nibs (optional)
1 tbsp nut butter (page 27)

Makes 2 servings

We couldn't write this book without including a milkshake. It wouldn't feel right. This chocolate version is made with coconut milk, which gives it a rich and creamy texture. We love making layered milkshakes and smoothies. They look prettier and make the drinking experience more interesting as the individual flavors slowly combine when you work your way down the shake. Blackberries and chocolate are perfect together, but raspberries would be really good as well.

Divide the blackberries between two glasses. Muddle them (mash them gently) in the bottom of the glasses. You can use a pestle or end of a rolling pin to do this. Put the rest of the ingredients in a blender and blend on high speed until frothy. Pour carefully into the glasses, making sure that the blackberries stay on the bottom, and serve immediately.

Tip: We often peel and slice ripe, leftover bananas and store them in a container in the freezer. They are great for making smoothies, and you don't need to add any ice.

Juicing

If you have never tried making your own juice, you are in for a real treat. Although you can make juice with a blender, we recommend using an electric juicer for the best results. You can juice most vegetables and it's a great way to increase your intake of vitamins and minerals. Since not all vegetables taste great on their own, we usually add some tanginess and sweetness. Lemon adds a fresh flavor to green vegetables like kale, broccoli and spinach. The vitamin C in the citrus also improves the body's ability to absorb the iron in those vegetables. Apple is one of the best fruits to juice. It has a very sweet flavor and releases a lot of juice.

Each serves 2

Choose a few fruits and vegetables from each group and you will get a good, balanced juice:

Vegetables:
  kale, broccoli, spinach, beet, carrot, fennel,
  bell pepper, cucumber, tomato, cauliflower,
  sweet potato, romaine, celery
Sweet fruits:
  apple, pear, melon, peach, plum, orange, cherries
Tangy fruits:
  lemon, grapefruit, lime, kiwi
Herbs:
  parsley, basil, lemon balm, mint
For a kick:
  ginger, horseradish, wheatgrass, licorice, turmeric, saffron

Virgin Apple Mojito

3 limes, chopped
10–15 mint leaves
1 apple
2 kiwi
1 cup soda water

Divide the limes and mint between two glasses and muddle (lightly crush) with a pestle. Press the apples and kiwi fruits through a juicer. Add the juice to the glasses, then add the soda water. For serving, add a few ice cubes and a straw to each glass.

Beet & Watermelon Juice

2 medium beets
½ small watermelon
1 handful of fresh mint, leaves picked

Press the ingredients through a juicer. Serve the juice in glasses with a few ice cubes and a straw in each.

Tips:
- Depending on the quality of your machine, leaf and grassy vegetables can be a little tricky to juice. A good tip is to roll them into a tight ball before adding them to the juicer.
- If you do not have a juicer, use a blender and strain the juice through a nut milk bag, cheesecloth or a fine sieve.
- If you find a combination that you like, turn it into a smoothie by adding milk, avocado, yogurt, banana, mango or frozen berries.
- You can easily make juices and smoothies into popsicles. Pour the mixture into ice pop molds, place a stick in each and freeze.

191　　　　　　　　　　　　　　　　　　　　DRINKS

Carrot & Grapefruit Juice

3 carrots
1 grapefruit
½ in piece of fresh ginger
1 eating apple
½ yellow bell pepper, seeded

Press the ingredients through a juicer.
Serve the juice in glasses with a few ice cubes and a straw in each.

Raspberry & Licorice Juice

2 eating apples
5 oz/1¼ cups raspberries
  (thawed if frozen)
1 tsp licorice powder (add after juicing)

Press the apples and raspberries through a juicer.
Add the licorice powder and stir. Serve the juice
in glasses with a few ice cubes and a straw in each.

Green Cleanse Power Shot

2 eating apples
½ in piece of fresh ginger
1 lemon
½ fennel bulb
1 tsp wheatgrass powder
a pinch of ground turmeric

Press the apples, ginger, lemon and fennel through a juicer.
Stir in the wheatgrass powder and turmeric. Serve the juice
in glasses with a few ice cubes and a straw in each.

Sweet Hazelnut Masala Chai

2 cinnamon sticks
6 whole cloves
6 cardamom pods, split
2 whole star anise
1 slice of fresh ginger
2 tbsp black or green tea leaves
1–2 tbsp palm sugar
1 cup hazelnut or almond milk
   (recipe on page 27), or use
   store-bought

Serves 4

*This hot tea is all about the spices.
We love how the scent of cinnamon,
star anise, cardamom and clove fills
our kitchen as the chai simmers on
the stove. We make it with our own
hazelnut milk, and it is just as good
on a hot summer day as it is on a dark
and cold winter evening.*

Combine 1 cup water with the spices in a saucepan and gently bring to a boil, then reduce the heat and simmer for 15 minutes. Remove from the heat, add the tea and palm sugar and steep for 5–7 minutes. Strain out the spices and tea and stir. Add the nut milk, reheat until barely simmering, then pour into cups and serve.

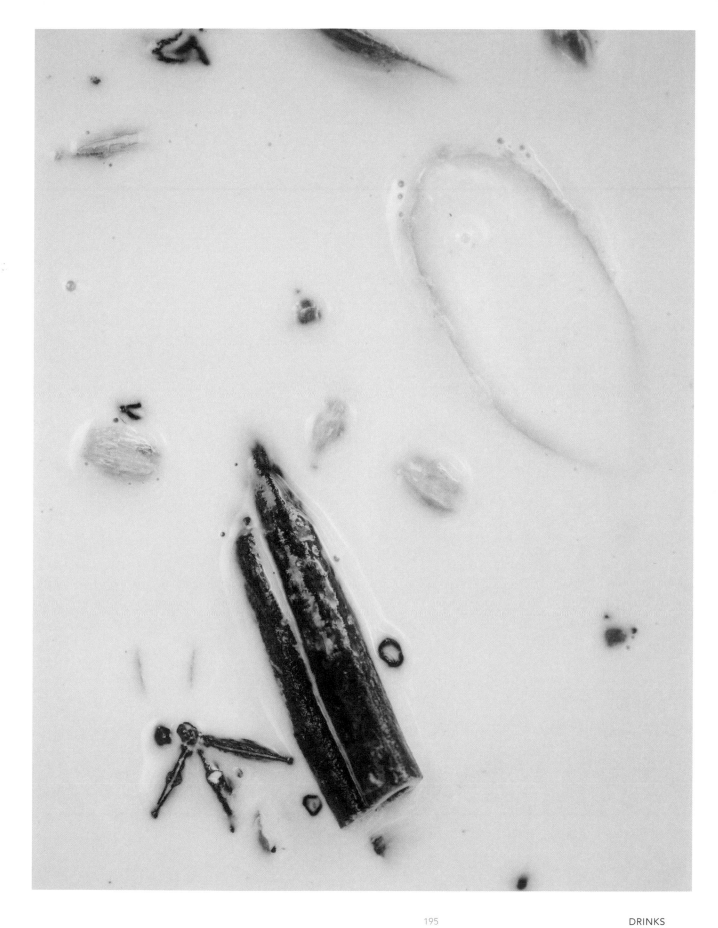

Smoothies

*As we mentioned earlier, we make smoothies almost every day.
They are different depending on the season and what we have in
our fridge, freezer and fruit basket. Here are two different versions.
The Wake-up Smoothie is quite elaborate, while the Classic Berry
Smoothie is simpler. We vary them by adding superfood powders,
seeds, nuts, pea or hemp protein powder and herbs.*

Each serves 2

Wake-up Smoothie

½ pineapple, peeled and cored
½ tsp green tea powder (instant)
5 broccoli florets
a handful of flat-leaf parsley
½ in piece of fresh ginger, peeled
1 cup unsweetened apple juice or water
  (depending on how sweet you prefer it)
3 ice cubes

Put all the ingredients in a blender and blend until nice and smooth.
Pour into 2 glasses and serve immediately.

Classic Berry Smoothie

4 oz/1 cup fresh berries (thawed if frozen)
4 tbsp dried goji berries
1 banana
1½ cups oat milk (page 27), or milk of your choice
1 tsp vanilla extract

Put all the ingredients in a blender and blend until nice and
smooth; add extra milk if you prefer it thinner. Pour into
2 glasses and serve immediately.

Saffron, Rosehip & Honey Lassi

1½ cups yogurt
2 tbsp honey
2 tsp rosehip powder (or ½ tsp
  ground cinnamon)
1 tsp bee pollen (optional)
½ tsp freshly ground cardamom seeds
2 pinches of saffron powder
a pinch of sea salt
2 ice cubes

Serves 2

In India they often drink lassi to accompany a meal. It's easy to understand why, since it's exactly what you need after a spicy curry. When we travelled around India we tried at least a dozen different versions. Apart from the traditional salted lassi and smoothie-like fruit lassis, they also use more complex flavors like rose water, honey or saffron. We have combined a few of those flavors in our version. You can buy rosehip powder in most healthfood stores; if you can't find it you can leave it out or use cinnamon instead.

Combine all the ingredients in a blender with 1½ cups water. Pulse until smooth, light and frothy. Taste and add more saffron if necessary. Pour into 2 large glasses and serve immediately.

Elderflower Lemonade

40 elderflower heads
3 lemons
1 cup honey

Makes 8½ cups lemonade

Elderflower has the most wonderful aroma. In the spring, the blossoming elder trees can be found everywhere around Stockholm – you can easily find a tree just by closing your eyes and following the scent. We don't, however, recommend picking elderflowers in very urban areas. Search outside the city if you can.

It has always been a mystery to us why all recipes drench the elderflowers in sugar. With their wonderful flavor, there is no need for such absurd quantities. Our lemonade is therefore half as sweet, but twice as flavorful.

Gently shake the elderflowers to get rid of any small bugs or dirt.
Cut the lemons into thin slices. In a wide, large pan or crock, arrange the elderflowers and lemon slices in layers. Bring 8½ cups water to a boil in a large saucepan. Add the honey and stir until dissolved, then pour over the elderflowers and lemon.
Leave to steep in a cool place for 48 hours, stirring once a day. Steep for longer, if you prefer a more concentrated flavor.
Strain the liquid by pouring it through a cheesecloth or muslin into a large bowl. Pour the strained lemonade through a funnel into clean bottles and refrigerate. Will keep for at least a few weeks unopened.
Serve with sparkling water, according to taste.

Tip: You can freeze the flowers and add them to smoothies, or make more lemonade later in the year.

Sweets & Treats

I have this strange habit, which I don't even think about, but that drives Luise crazy. Apparently I always leave a small piece of whatever I cook/bake/ eat behind. It can be two spoonfuls of salad in a bowl, four strawberries in the box, or a tablespoon of flour in the bag when I am baking. My own theory is that I think it is good to save it for later. But truth be told, we only end up with ridiculously small portions of leftovers, and half empty bags of flour in the pantry. Hopefully, if you try any of the sweets and treats in this chapter, there will be no leftovers. Our fingers are crossed that you and your family will lick the bowls, ask for second servings, and reach for the last piece.

All our desserts are sweetened with natural sweeteners, baked with whole grains, and here and there we have even added some vegetables to them. Our intention has never been to make anything less indulgent than you are used to. In our opinion, a cake that combines the subtle aroma of earthy red beets with dark decadent chocolate, the soft texture of spelt flour and the toasty tones from maple syrup, is far more intriguing than any sugar-and-flour cake on the market. We are all about natural flavors and hope we can get you hooked, whether you are trying our cold berry soup, cardamom flavored buns or double chocolate raspberry brownies.

– *David*

Cardamom & Apple Buns

4 tbsp (½ stick) unsalted butter, or
  coconut oil
1 cup soy milk (or milk of your choice)
5 tbsp honey or maple syrup
1 tbsp active dry yeast
2 cups light spelt flour
1 cup whole-grain spelt flour
1½ tsp cardamom seeds,
  freshly ground
a pinch of sea salt

FILLING
4 tbsp (½ stick) unsalted butter,
  at room temperature, or coconut oil
½ cup unsweetened applesauce
1 eating apple, grated, excess
  moisture squeezed out
2 tbsp shredded dried coconut
1½ tsp cardamom seeds,
  freshly ground
1 egg, beaten, for the glaze

Makes around 15 buns

I remember my grandmother standing in her farm kitchen with a rolling pin in her hand and a double batch of cinnamon buns ready to be rolled out on a floured table. I also remember eating those buns hot from the oven. Not much could make a 6-year-old boy happier. We came up with a bun recipe that has all the same qualities but is a healthier version of traditional cardamom buns. Since these buns aren't super sweet, we added more filling to compensate. We also updated the flavors by adding apple, coconut and freshly ground cardamom. If you make these, you have to eat the first bun hot from the oven. There is nothing quite like it.
– David

Melt the butter in a saucepan, add the milk and honey and heat until the temperature is lukewarm, about 100°F. Pour into a large bowl and stir in the yeast until it is dissolved.

Sift the flours together and add about two-thirds of it to the milk mixture. Sprinkle the cardamom and salt over. Mix to a dough. Gradually knead in enough of the remaining flour just until soft and no longer sticky. Do not over-knead. Cover and leave to rise in a warm place for about an hour, or until doubled in size.

On a floured surface, roll and stretch the dough to a rectangle, about 20 x 18 in wide and about ¼ in thick.

Spread the butter and applesauce evenly across the whole dough and sprinkle on the grated apple, coconut and cardamom. Carefully lift one long edge of the dough (closest to you) and fold it two-thirds of the way up, then fold down the top third. Now you should have a rectangle that is roughly 20 x 6 in. Use a sharp knife to cut the dough into roughly 1 ¼ in wide strips.

Take each strip and carefully (so the filling doesn't fall out) stretch and twist them three times and tie into loose knot-shaped buns, with the ends tucked into the middle. Put on a baking sheet lined with parchment paper, cover with a kitchen towel, and leave to rise for 30 minutes. Preheat the oven to 425°F. Brush the buns with the egg glaze and bake for 10–12 minutes, until golden.

Tip: Spelt flour does not require much kneading to develop the gluten, so be careful not to overwork the dough.

Decadent Beet & Chocolate Cake

⅔ cup extra virgin olive oil
⅓ cup maple syrup or honey
2 oz/⅓ cup dark chocolate (75% cocoa solids) broken into pieces
scant 2 cups peeled and grated beets (about 3–4 medium)

3 large eggs
1¾ cups light spelt flour
2 tsp baking powder
5 tbsp cocoa powder
a pinch of sea salt
1 tbsp shredded dried coconut

Serves 10

I have been baking chocolate cakes since I was a teenager. In fact, for a few years I religiously baked chocolate cakes two or three times a week, so I see myself as pretty experienced in this area. Although this cake is far less sweetened than the chocolate cakes I made as a teenager, it has so much more flavor. Don't be intimidated by the beet. They don't taste strange at all; instead, they actually add more depth and dimension to the chocolate.
– David

Preheat the oven to 350°F.

Warm the oil in a saucepan over very low heat. Add the maple syrup and chocolate and stir until the chocolate is melted. Remove from the heat.

Add the grated beets and stir to combine. Beat the eggs in a small bowl and add them to the saucepan.

In a separate bowl, sift the flour, baking powder, cocoa powder and salt together and stir into the beet mixture.

Grease a 10 in bundt pan or a cake pan with a little oil. Sprinkle the sides of the pan with the shredded coconut, to prevent the batter from sticking. Pour in the cake batter and bake for 25–30 minutes, or until slightly dark and cracked on top and still a little sticky inside.

Leave to cool for 15 minutes before carefully removing the cake from the pan. It tastes amazing while warm, but can be cooled and kept in the fridge for 2–3 days.

Carrot, Coconut & Banana Cupcakes

⅓ cup (5 tbsp plus 1 tsp) unsalted butter
4 tbsp maple syrup or agave syrup
1 tsp cardamom seeds, freshly ground
1 tsp ground cinnamon
1 tsp ground allspice
½ vanilla bean or ½ tsp vanilla extract
5 oz/1½ cups almonds, ground
½ cup chickpea flour (or another gluten-free flour)
½ cup shredded dried coconut
2 tsp baking powder
1⅓ cups grated carrots (about 4)

1 large ripe banana
4 large egg whites

FROSTING
7 oz/scant 1 cup cream cheese, softened
3 tbsp honey
juice of ½ lime
15 hazelnuts, toasted and coarsely chopped

Makes about 12 cupcakes

These cupcakes are filled with wonderful warm spices. The scent of cardamom, cinnamon and allspice wafts from the oven as they bake. We only use egg whites and not very much flour in this recipe, which makes them very light and airy. Muffins and cupcakes always taste best freshly baked. If you are having a party you can of course make them a day in advance, but nothing beats the taste when they are fresh from the oven.

Preheat the oven to 350°F. Line a muffin pan with 12 paper muffin cups. Melt the butter on low heat in a small saucepan. Add the maple syrup, all the spices and the vanilla and stir well. Set aside to infuse for 10 minutes.

Put the almonds in a mixing bowl and add the flour, coconut and baking powder.

Put the grated carrots and banana in a blender and blend until the banana is completely mashed and incorporated with the carrots (you can also do this step by hand). Add to the mixing bowl and stir well to combine with the dry ingredients.

Beat the egg whites until soft peaks form. Fold into the cupcake mixture and then add the spice-infused butter and stir until smooth. Spoon into the muffin cups and bake for 25–30 minutes or until golden.

Meanwhile, make the frosting. Beat together the cream cheese, honey and lime juice in a small bowl.

Let the muffins cool on a wire rack before spooning or piping on the frosting. Decorate with coarsely chopped hazelnuts.

Simple Chocolate Mousse

2 ripe avocados, halved, pitted and peeled
3 ripe bananas
⅓ cup nut butter (see page 27 for recipe)
¼ cup cocoa powder
2 tbsp carob powder (or more cocoa)
2 tbsp hemp seeds (optional)
a pinch of sea salt
fresh berries, to serve

Serves 4

This vegan chocolate mousse is pretty far from the traditional kind. First of all, it is ridiculously simple, taking no more than three minutes to make. None of the common ingredients (heavy cream, chocolate, eggs, butter) are used – instead the creaminess and sweetness come from avocados, bananas, nut butter and cocoa powder. We usually use almond butter, but when we don't have it at home we also use peanut butter or hazelnut butter.

Combine all of the mousse ingredients in a blender or food processor. Purée for about 30 seconds or until it reaches a mousse-like consistency. Scoop into glasses or small coffee cups and chill in the fridge for 30 minutes.
Serve topped with fresh berries.

Tip: Cocoa and carob powder complete each other, both in taste and nutritional values. Cocoa is rich in magnesium and carob is rich in calcium.

SWEETS AND TREATS

Double Chocolate Raspberry Brownie

25 fresh medjool dates, pitted
¼ cup coconut oil
2 tbsp maple syrup
⅓ cup cocoa powder
2 tea bags raspberry leaf herbal tea
  (we use Clipper or Yogi), cut open
½ tsp sea salt
5 oz/1¼ cups coarsely chopped walnuts

CHOCOLATE TOPPING
¼ cup soft coconut oil
2 tbsp maple syrup
⅓ cup cocoa powder
fresh raspberries, to serve

Serves 6

This is a dressed-up alternative to our raw Spirulena Chocolate Truffles on page 232. Although delicious as a treat, those truffles might not be pretty enough to qualify as a dessert after dinner. Therefore we created this more elaborate version with a raspberry leaf flavor and melted chocolate topping. We also do a winter version of this by substituting the raspberry leaf tea with chai tea.

Grease six 4 in springform cake pans or one large 9 in springform cake pan with coconut oil.

Purée all the brownie ingredients, except the walnuts, in a food processor with 2 tbsp water. If your food processor isn't powerful enough to purée all the ingredients at the same time, you can divide it into three different batches and then combine them afterwards.

Add the nuts and combine the mixture by hand. Divide the mixture between the cake pans (or put it into the large pan). Rub a little coconut oil on your hands to prevent the mixture from sticking, then use your fingers to flatten out the mixture in the pans. It should be about ½ in deep. Put the pans in the fridge and leave to set for at least 30 minutes. If covered, they will keep in the fridge for a couple of days.

At the end of the chilling time, start making the chocolate topping. Melt the coconut oil and maple syrup on low heat in a small saucepan. Add the cocoa powder while stirring.

Remove the brownies from the fridge. Pour the chocolate topping over and serve immediately, so your guests can watch the chocolate as it sets. It usually takes about 2 minutes. Top with a few raspberries, carefully remove from the springform pans and, well, dig in!

Tip: We often use herbal teas instead of spices when we need flavors that can be a bit tricky to find. Chamomile, chai, peppermint and rosehip are herbal teas that add interesting flavors to desserts, soups and breads.

Frozen Strawberry Cheesecake on a Sunflower Crust

2½ cups sunflower seeds
2 tbsp hemp seeds (optional)
12 fresh medjool dates, pitted
2 tbsp coconut oil
½ tsp sea salt

FILLING
2 cups fresh strawberries (or frozen unsweetened strawberries)
juice of ½ lemon

½ cup honey or agave syrup
2 oz/2 cups quark (or Greek yogurt or mascarpone)

TOPPING
1 cup strawberries
a few edible flowers (see tip)

Serves 8–10

I don't think we have ever served this cake to someone who hasn't immediately loved it. Therefore it has become one of our go-to recipes for all kinds of occasions. We often make it with nuts in the crust, but lately we have moved to this seed-based crust. It has the most wonderful flavor and texture, not to mention that it is allergy-friendly and gluten-free. Since the crust is very sweet, the filling doesn't have to be. If you are looking for new variations, you can play around with all kinds of yogurts, soft cheeses or coconut creams. You can also vary the color of the filling by adding different berries to it. If you are having a big party make a rainbow of colors: blueberry blue, kiwi green, mango yellow and so on.

Toast the sunflower seeds in a frying pan on low heat, or on a baking sheet in a 350°F oven for 6–8 minutes. Let cool for a few minutes before putting them into a food processor or blender together with the hemp seeds. Pulse for about 20 seconds. The seeds should be chopped but not powdered. Add the dates, coconut oil and salt and process until the mixture comes together to form a sticky crust. Alternatively, mash the dates until caramel-smooth and work in the remaining ingredients. Put the mixture into an 8 in springform cake pan and flatten it out over the base. Chill in the fridge while you prepare the filling.

Purée the strawberries, lemon juice and honey in a food processor or blender, pour into a large bowl and add the quark. Mix well. Pour the mixture on top of the crust in the cake pan and put it in the freezer for about 1½ hours. You can keep it in the freezer for a few days but you will need to let it thaw for about 20 minutes before serving.

Top the cake with strawberries and a couple of flowers.
Serve immediately.

Tip: Here are some suggestions for edible flowers: violas, calendula, roses, rosehip, dandelions, carnations, lavender, cornflowers, pea flowers, day lilies and chamomile. Although the flowers are edible we mainly use them for decoration.

Tip: For vegans, substitute vegan cream cheese for quark.

SWEETS AND TREATS

Fruit Roll-Ups

RED RASPBERRY ROLLS
- 10½ oz/2½ cups raspberries, fresh or frozen and thawed
- 1 banana, peeled and cut into chunks
- 1 tbsp unsweetened applesauce

YELLOW MANGO ROLLS
- 1 large mango, peeled, pitted and cut into chunks
- 2 oranges, peeled
- 10 dried unsulphured apricots (pitted)

Makes 2 trays/40 roll-ups

They look, feel and taste like sweets, but the only ingredient in our roll-ups is fruit. We have taken these to a couple of birthday parties for Elsa's friends and they have always been a hit. Here are two recipes, but you can create endless color and flavor combinations by changing the fruit. They need about 5–6 hours in the oven on the lowest temperature, so we usually make two or three batches at a time. If you have a dehydrator, now is the time to use it. Pour the purée onto your Teflex-lined dehydrator trays. Spread evenly until about ¼ inch thick. Dehydrate for 6–7 hours at 115°F or until completely dry. Peel off the Teflex.

Prepare the raspberry rolls. Add the raspberries, banana and applesauce to a blender or food processor. Purée on high speed until smooth. Taste it and add more sweet fruit (applesauce or banana) if needed. Now check the consistency – you should be able to pour the purée, but it should be thick enough to stay where you pour it. Add some orange juice or water if it is too thick and more fruit if it is too thin.

Preheat the oven to its lowest setting. Line two baking sheets with nonstick parchment paper or silicone baking mats if you have them. Pour the purée onto one of the sheets – 2¼ cups fruit purée should be enough to cover it. Spread it out evenly with a spatula – this is very important; otherwise the rolls will end up too dry in one spot and too wet in another. It should be about ¼ in thick. Now prepare the mango rolls in the same way and spread onto the other prepared baking sheet. Put in the oven. Open the oven door once an hour to let the moisture out and switch positions of the trays. They are ready when the purée isn't sticky anymore and can be separated from the parchment paper, normally after 5–6 hours, depending on your oven.

We carefully remove them from the parchment paper before cutting them, since we think it looks prettier, but you could also leave the paper on, and peel it off when you eat them. Use scissors or a sharp knife to cut them into 1 x 6 in strips and roll them up. Store in an airtight container in a cool place for up to a month.

Cantaloupe Granita with Lemon & Mint

3 oz cantaloupe melon
juice of ½ lemon
½ cup pure apple juice (or syrup,
    but then use less)
10 mint leaves

Serves 4–6

When I met David in Rome we often went out for a lemon granita. It is a typically Italian dessert that is very refreshing in the summer heat or after a heavy dinner. It is actually also easy to make yourself. You will need to whisk it into the right texture, but apart from that your freezer does all the work. And if you use seasonally sweet fruit, no sugar is needed.

– Luise

Cut the melon in half, discard the seeds and scoop out the flesh with a spoon. Put it into a blender or food processor, together with the rest of the ingredients. Pulse until everything is completely puréed. Taste it and make sure that the fruit is sweet enough. If not, add more apple juice. Pour into a shallow container, cover with a lid, and freeze. After about an hour it is time to open the lid and whisk the mixture with a fork. You want to break up any ice crystals that form. Put it back in the freezer. Whisk again every 30 minutes during the next 3 hours. Now it should have the typical granita texture and is ready to be served.
You can keep it in the freezer for a few days, but remember to check on it and every now and then and whisk with a fork, so it maintains the right texture.

Hemp Protein Bars

DRY MIXTURE

1 cup pumpkin seeds
generous 1 cup shredded dried coconut
½ cup hemp seeds
½ cup hemp protein powder
  (or more hemp seeds)
½ cup chia seeds
2 tbsp bee pollen (optional)

WET MIXTURE

20 fresh medjool dates, pitted
⅓ cup coconut oil
¼ cup cocoa powder
1 tsp vanilla extract

⅓ cup rolled oats
2 tbsp poppy seeds

Makes around 15 bars

This is one of the most appreciated and commented upon recipes on our blog. The bars are not only really tasty as a midday snack for all ages, but we also wrap them in paper to eat after we have been working out. They are sweet in a very nice and nourishing way and packed with protein.

In a food processor or high-speed blender, combine all of the dry ingredients and pulse quickly. Do not overprocess, as you want it a little crunchy. Place the mixture in a bowl and set aside.

Add the dates, coconut oil, cocoa powder and vanilla to the food processor or high-speed blender and purée. This might take some time. If your blender isn't powerful enough, you might have to help out by stirring a few times with a fork or add a dash of water.

Pour the wet ingredients over the dry ingredients, add the oats and poppy seeds and stir until well combined.

Spread the batter into an 11 x 7 in baking pan lined with parchment paper and press down the mixture so it is compact. Chill in the fridge for about 30 minutes.

Cut into bars, wrap them in paper and store in an airtight container. Keep for around a week in the fridge.

Tip: If you do not have a high-speed blender, place your pitted dates on a plate and mash with a fork until they are sticky and smooth as caramel; it'll take a few minutes. Then add the remaining ingredients one by one and knead by hand until well combined.

SWEETS AND TREATS

Vanilla Peaches with Pistachio Crumble

5 ripe peaches
4 tbsp dry vermouth
4 tbsp honey
1 vanilla bean
⅓ cup shelled pistachios,
   finely chopped
vanilla ice cream, yogurt or
   mascarpone, to serve

Serves 5

When I was a kid my dad used to set bananas on fire in the frying pan by pouring alcohol on them. It was a little stunt he had and we were madly impressed every time. We asked him to do it often, even though we actually weren't too fond of the taste of the bananas. Today I have grown to love those flavors. I don't set my peaches on fire, but I think they make a pretty good dessert anyway.
– David

Preheat the oven to 400°F.

Cut each peach in half and remove the pit. Place the halves on a baking sheet, cut-side up.

Put the vermouth and honey in a small bowl. Cut the vanilla pod in half lengthwise, scrape out the seeds and add to the bowl. Whisk until combined. Add the pistachios to the bowl and stir.

Scoop a teaspoon of the honey-drenched nuts into the pit of each peach. Drizzle the remaining nut mixture over the peaches, until they are all covered. Bake for about 20 minutes, or until very soft and slightly golden.

Serve with vanilla ice cream, yogurt or mascarpone.

Cold Red Berry Soup with Cream

3 oz ripe red berries (such as strawberries, raspberries, red currants, lingonberries)
1 vanilla bean, seeds scraped, or 2 tsp vanilla extract
25 fresh medjool dates, pitted
1½ cups nut cream of your choice (page 27), for serving

Serves 4–6

Although David is pretty good at speaking Danish, there is one sentence he will never manage to pronounce like a true Dane. It's the name of this soup: Rødgrød med fløde. *It's just one of those impossible Danish sentences. The exact translation is actually red porridge with cream, but it is more like a thick soup than a porridge. Regardless of the name, it is the perfect summer treat on a hot day. Our version is quite different from the traditional, since we use the thickness of dates and the whole berries instead of adding sugar and starch.*
– Luise

Place the berries, vanilla and 1 cup water in a saucepan. Bring slowly to a simmer over low heat. Mash the pitted dates with a fork on a plate until smooth and add to the pan. Simmer for about 10 minutes – the berries and dates should almost have dissolved.

Remove from the heat and purée the soup with a hand/immersion blender. Place a fine sieve over a large bowl in the sink. Pour the soup through it so all the seeds are strained. Use the back of a spoon to help the thick soup through. This takes a couple of minutes.

Place the soup in the fridge for a few hours until completely cold.

Serve in deep plates or bowls with cream (oat, nut, coconut or cow's) drizzled on top.

Spirulina Chocolate Truffles

20 large fresh medjool dates, pitted
2 tbsp extra virgin coconut oil
2 tbsp shredded dried coconut
2 tbsp cocoa powder
1 tbsp spirulina powder or wheatgrass
   powder

ROLL IN
   10 almonds, coarsely chopped,
      or 3 tbsp shredded dried coconut
      or 3 tbsp cocoa powder

Serves 5

When we want a quick treat we often make raw truffles by blending fresh dates with nuts or seeds, various spices and cocoa powder. It's a simple, no-fail recipe that we adjust to whatever we have in our pantry. They are perfect as an evening treat or a mid-day snack. Sometimes we also make them extra pretty by rolling them in different toppings, and give them as gifts. The rolling process is Elsa's favorite part.

Spirulina is a superfood that can be difficult to use because of its algae taste, but this recipe is so full of flavor that the nutritious spirulina just blends right in.

Place the dates on a plate and mash with a fork until they are sticky and smooth as caramel. You can also use a food processor for this step. Add the rest of the ingredients and knead (or pulse) until mixed well. Place the mixture in the fridge for about 10 minutes. Use your hands to form 15–20 round truffles; they should be half the size of a golf ball. Roll the truffles in chopped almonds, dried coconut or cocoa powder and chill in the fridge for 20 minutes before serving.

233   SWEETS AND TREATS

Summer Berry Pancake Cake

PANCAKE BATTER
- 1¾ cups buckwheat flour
- 3 large eggs
- 2 cups oat milk (page 27), or milk of your choice
- 1 tbsp coconut oil, plus more for frying
- a pinch of sea salt

LAYERS
- 2 cups thick cream (cow's, oat or soy), chilled

- 3 ripe bananas, thinly sliced
- 8 oz/2 cups raspberries, mashed with a fork
- 8 oz/1½ cups blackberries, mashed with a fork
- ⅔ cup nut butter (page 27)
- ½ cup date syrup (page 30)

TOPPING
- 5 oz/1¼ cups raspberries
- 4 oz/1 cup blackberries
- 2 tbsp chopped pistachio nuts

Serves 10

I have made different versions of this cake since I was a child, and I never get tired of it. I think it is so beautiful with all those stacks of pancakes, and the berries and cream squishing out from the sides. Traditionally, you put jam between the layers, but we stick to fresh fruit, nut butter and date syrup. The pancakes should be very thin, so we always use a nonstick frying pan when we make these. You can prepare the pancakes one day in advance and assemble the cake just before serving.
– David

To make the batter, add all the ingredients, plus 1 cup water to a large mixing bowl and whisk vigorously until you have a smooth batter. Make sure that there are no lumps of flour left. Refrigerate for 20 minutes. Give it a good whisk after you have removed it from the fridge, as the flour tends to sink to the bottom.

Heat an 8 in, preferably nonstick, frying pan on medium-high heat. When the pan is hot, add a few drops of oil and about ⅓ cup of the batter. Tilt the pan until the batter is evenly distributed. Fry for 45–60 seconds on each side, until the pancakes are golden and can be flipped easily with a spatula. Fry all of the pancakes – the batter should make about 15 – and place on parchment paper to cool. You can layer with parchment paper between the pancakes to prevent them from sticking together.

To assemble, pour the cold cream into a large chilled bowl. Use an electric hand mixer or a whisk to whip it until soft peaks form. Set aside. Put the cold first pancake on a cake stand. Spread a layer of thin slices of banana evenly over the top. Add another pancake and top it with about a third of the mashed raspberries. Then continue with the next pancake and a third of the mashed blackberries. Continue with another pancake and carefully spread a thin layer of nut butter and date syrup on it. Add another pancake and spread with a layer of whipped cream. Then start all over with the banana layer. Continue until all the pancakes are covered. Top with whipped cream, fresh fruit and finely chopped pistachios.

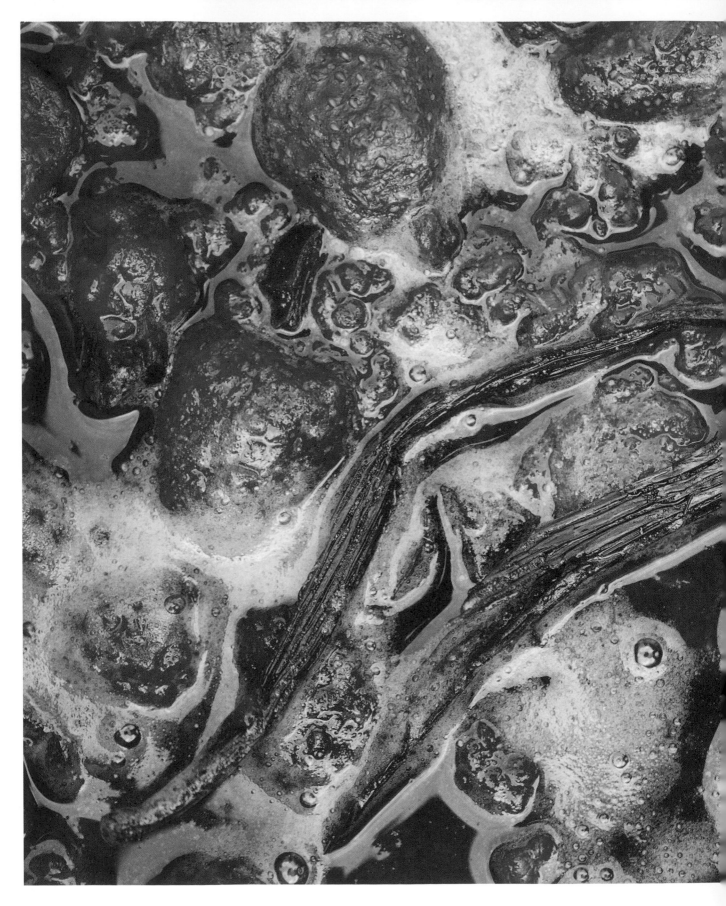

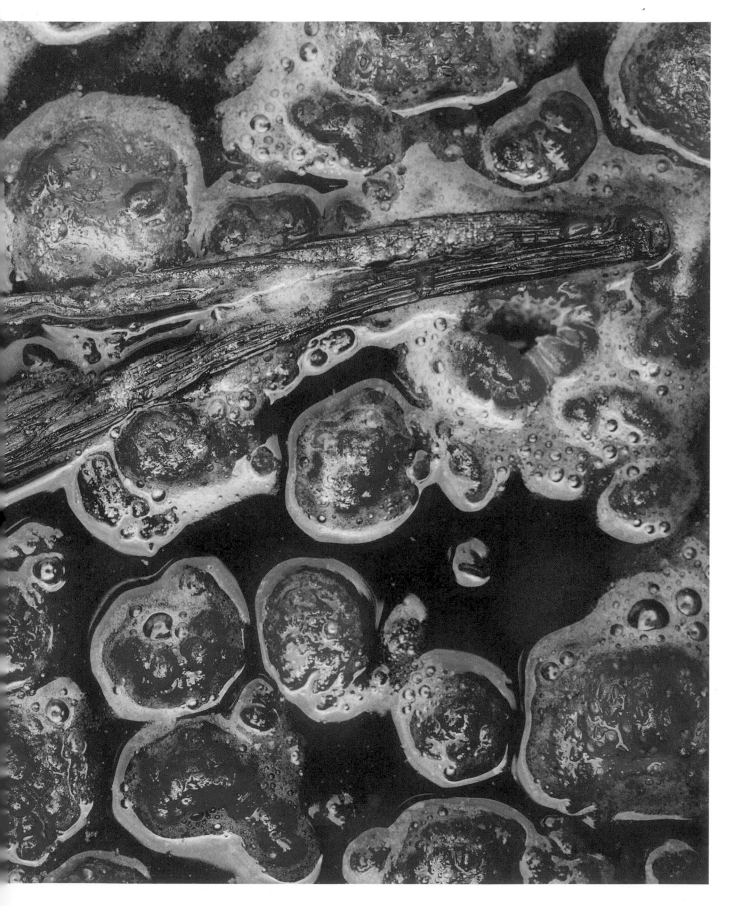

SWEETS AND TREATS

INDEX

flour-free banana & coconut pancakes 45

Sicilian parmigiana di zucchine 136

see also frittata; omelets

elderflower lemonade 203

F

falafels

baked herb & pistachio falafel 65

fennel

fennel & coconut tart 96

green cleanse power shot 193

lemony fennel & lentil salad 84

fermented essentials *13*

feta cheese

quinoa & cauliflower cakes with ramps 71

savoury corn & millet muffins 95

fig, rhubarb & pear compôte 160

fillings

apple & mushroom filling 100

corn & mango filling 82

orange quinoa filling 98

purple beet filling 98

flax oil 7

flax seeds *8*

flours *11*

frittata, herb & asparagus 38

frosting & icing

chocolate topping 217

cream cheese frosting 213

fruit

buckwheat & ginger porridge 57

fruit roll-ups 222

juicing 188

stone fruit salad with creamy goat cheese 40

see also berries

G

gazpacho, strawberry 108

ghee (clarified butter) 7, 25

ginger, pickled 132

goat cheese

beet, apple & goat cheese wraps 98

green zucchini topping 143

lemony fennel & lentil salad 84

stone fruit salad with creamy goat cheese 40

white potato topping 143

goat's milk 9

goji *12*

grains *11*

sprouting 28

granitas

cantaloupe granita with lemon & mint 225

granola, flowered 51

grapefruit

carrot & grapefruit juice 193

grapes

wild rice, sunchoke & grape salad 76

guacamole 118

H

halloumi cheese

amaranth & halloumi-stuffed tomatoes 152

haricot beans 9

hash pan with fava beans 129

hazelnut milk

sweet hazelnut masala chai 194

hazelnuts *8*

broccoli pesto 175

hazelnut, eggplant & mushroom parcels 126

hemp milk 9

hemp protein powder *12*

hemp seeds *8*

T

tacos
    savory tacos with corn & mango filling 82
tagine, Moroccan vegetable 125
tamari *13*
tarts, savory
    fennel & coconut tart 96
tea
    sweet hazelnut masala chai 194
tea, green
    wake-up smoothie 197
tofu *9*
    sushi explosion with wasabi yogurt 132–3
    tom kha tofu 66
tomatoes
    amaranth & halloumi stuffed tomatoes 152
    apple ketchup 30
    basic tomato sauce 22
    cashew & tomato dressing 131
    red Sicilian topping 142
    roasted tomato & chickpea soup 81
    sage & walnut pâté 173
    Sicilian parmigiana di zucchine 136
    tomato chili salsa 65
tortillas *see* wraps
truffles, spirulina chocolate 232

U

udon rice *10*

V

vanilla *10*
vegetable stock 22
vegetables
    hash pan with fava beans 129
    juicing 188
    mashed roots 149
    Moroccan vegetable tagine 125
    roasted roots 152
    spicy skinny root sticks 178
    sushi explosion with wasabi yogurt 132–3
vinegar 7

W

walnuts 8
    sage & walnut pâté *173*
wasabi yogurt 132–3
watermelon
    beet & watermelon juice 189
    strawberry gazpacho 108
wheat berry *12*
wheat germ *11*
wheatgrass powder *13*
white wine vinegar 7
wild rice, sunchoke & grape salad 76
wraps
    beet, apple & goat cheese wraps 98

Y

yeast *11*
yellow-eyed beans *8–9*
yogurt
    raita 89
    saffron, rosehip & honey lassi 200
    super simple yogurt 25
    wasabi yogurt 132–3

TACK. TAK. THANK YOU!

Elsa – you can't read this just yet but you have been stirring the bowls, playing in the grass and running around our legs while we have been trying recipes and taking the photos for this book. If you hadn't been such a miraculously happy child, we would never have landed this project on such a tight schedule. Maybe you will pick this book up 10 years from now and read this. You probably won't remember it, but you were part of this project. We love you.

Johanna – all the photos in the book are wonderful! It's not always easy to work with your brother, but you did an amazing job balancing on tables and patiently waiting for the perfect light. We are such big fans of your work and really happy that you wanted to be our photographer.

Kate and Chris – we had no idea how to do a cookbook. Thank you for holding our hands throughout this process. And for believing in us and staying positive through all our concerns and doubts.

To all our family in Denmark and Sweden – we can't thank you enough for your loving support and for helping us out with everything from trying a rye bread recipe or loaning your car, to teaching us how to roll a cinnamon bun like Grandma.

Affe and Marie, Erik and Hanna, Kristina, Stefan and Inga, and Anders – thank you for lending your summer houses to us while we worked on this book. Your houses, gardens, furniture, tableware and doors (!) made amazing settings and backgrounds for our photos. Plus, we had a great time there.

And to all our amazing blog readers. It is your constant support, constructive recipe feedback and cheering comments that motivate us to grow and improve our kitchen skills. Some of you also helped us testing the recipes in this book. A big thank you to (hope we haven't forgotten anyone now):
Katie Dalebout, Jacquelyn Scoggin, Emily Meagher, Wendy Kastner, Line Sander Johansen, Elizabeth Allen, Michealla Redeker, Marijke Fisser, Matt & Amalie, Rikke Bülow Mindegaard Christensen, Natalia Mrukowicz, Susanne Irmer, Lisa Frenkel, Lydia Loeskow Söderberg, Helena Strand, Shadya Ghemati, Michèle Janse van Rensburg, Dana Slatkin, Yasmin Mckenzie, Anna Hastie, Blaine Tacker, Hjørdis Petersen, Jeanine Donofrio, Laura Gates, Sasha Gora, Modini Therese Natland, Sophie Pronovost, Klelia Shoo-Kara, Meg Pell, Benedikte Capion, Nicola Griffiths and Eveline Johnsson.
Tack. Tak. Thank you!

David Frenkiel and Luise Vindahl are the couple
behind the critically acclaimed vegetarian food blog
Green Kitchen Stories, which has followers from
all over the world. Healthy, seasonal and delicious
vegetarian recipes paired with colorful and beautiful
photos have become trademarks of their style.
Their work has appeared in *Saveur, Bon Appetit,
Gourmet, Cook Vegetarian, ELLE, Babble* and *Jamie
Oliver's Food Revolution*. Their app "Green Kitchen"
was selected as App of the Year Runner-Up in App
Store Best of 2012.
David is Swedish and Luise is Danish, and they
currently live in Stockholm with their daughter Elsa.
Apart from doing freelance recipe development and
photography, David works as a magazine art director
and Luise is studying to become a nutritional therapist.
This is their first cookbook.

www.greenkitchenstories.com

First published in the United States of America in 2013
by Rizzoli Publications, Inc.
300 Park Avenue South
New York, NY 10010
www.rizzoliusa.com

ISBN 978-0-8478-3960-5

Commissioning Editor: Kate Pollard, Hardie Grant
Coordinating Editor: Christopher Steighner, Rizzoli
Art Direction and design: Charlotte Heal
Photography and retouching: Johanna Frenkiel
Colour reproduction by p2D

Printed and bound China by 1010 Printing International Limited

2014 2015 2016 / 10 9 8 7 6 5 4 3 2

Library of Congress Control Number: 2013930299